stitch

stitch

Contemporary New Zealand Textile Artists

Ann Packer

RANDOM HOUSE
NEW ZEALAND

Acknowledgements

This book would never have happened without the input of a great many people. My thanks
to Jenny Hellen, Nic McCloy and the team at Random House for stitching it all up; to Louise
Day, Malcolm Harrison, Kristin Hollis, Claire Regnault and Anne Scott for their professional
input; to Jo and Georgie for the portraits; to Glenda and the team at Croydon Studios for their
photography; to Genevieve Packer for the cover; to Mike Chatterley of Ace Rentals for the cars;
to Anna and Sarah for Tuesday nights; to Jan, Helen, Kristin, Robyn and my dad, Harley for their
hospitality; and to my family for all their love and support.

Ann Packer

National Library of New Zealand Cataloguing-in-Publication Data

Packer, Ann, 1947-
Stitch: contemporary New Zealand textile artists / by Ann
Packer.
Includes bibliographical references and index.
ISBN-13: 978-1-86941-788-8
ISBN-10: 1-86941-788-7
1. Textile artists—New Zealand. 2. Textile crafts—New Zealand.
3. Fiberwork—New Zealand.
746.092293—dc 22

A RANDOM HOUSE BOOK
published by
Random House New Zealand
18 Poland Road, Glenfield, Auckland
www.randomhouse.co.nz

First published 2006

©2006 text: Ann Packer; images: Random House/the artist
        unless credited otherwise on page 251

The moral rights of the author have been asserted

ISBN-13: 978 1 86941 788 8
ISBN-10: 1 86941 788 7

Cover and text design: Sharon Grace, Grace Design
Front cover artwork: Genevieve Packer
Back cover artwork: Heeni Kerekere
Printed in China

To all who have so generously shared stories and stitches with me, especially Isabel McIlwraith, still stitching in her 100th year . . . my grateful thanks.

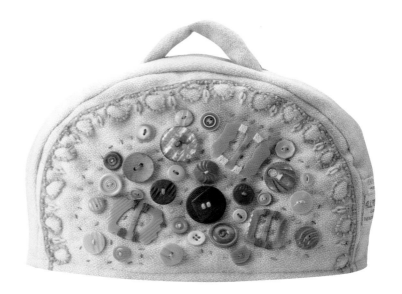

Contents

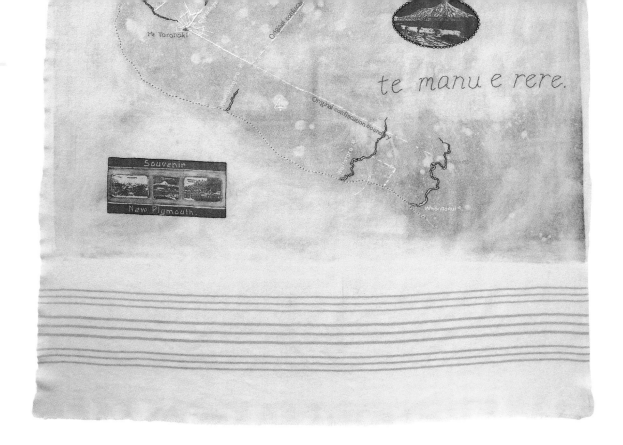

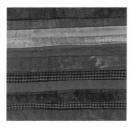  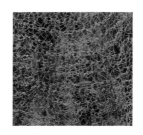 

Introduction

TEXTILE ARTS HAVE A HUGE
FOLLOWING IN NEW ZEALAND AT
GRASS ROOTS LEVEL, YET THERE IS
LITTLE TO REFLECT THIS IN OUR
GALLERIES AND BOOKS. *STITCH* IS
THE FIRST PUBLICATION IN FIFTEEN
YEARS DEDICATED TO THE WORK
OF AOTEAROA'S CONTEMPORARY
TEXTILE ARTISTS.

he pulling power of 'soft stuff' is
seen in record-breaking attendances
of exhibits such as Malcolm
Harrison's *The Family* — on tour
yet again, in 2006, from The Dowse — and over
twenty exhibitions around Auckland during
the 2005 National Quilt Symposium. Yet, with
the exception of The Dowse in Lower Hutt,
and Pataka, Porirua, there are few public art
institutions where you can regularly expect to see
quilts, costumes or cloaks on show.

Humans need textiles; we are wrapped in
cloth from cradle to grave. Textiles are among
the oldest surviving artefacts, pre-dating pottery
in archaeological terms. They have been used for
thousands of years, not only for clothing but also
for comfort, protection and shelter.

Textiles soften the hard edges of our lives
and our homes. Even the most pared-back,
minimalist interior needs soft touches — the
harder the style, the softer the textiles. From
possum fur to knitted blankets, current interior
design includes some very soft furnishings indeed.

The artists in this book come from a great
diversity of backgrounds. Some are young
and wildly enthusiastic, some are seasoned
practitioners. Some are immigrants from other
cultures, some Pakeha New Zealanders from
several generations, some tangata whenua. Some

refer to tradition, some crack it wide open. Some are highly trained in terms of technology, design and art history, some self-taught, and yet others learned their skills at the feet of their elders. All have a consuming passion for fabric and fibre.

They tell their stories with felted fibres, painted sheers, recycled blankets. They dye wool, flax, silk and cotton with synthetics, plant dyes and mud. They knit, hook, tuft, and needle- and machine-stitch. They create beautiful, weird and sometimes challenging objects that speak of the past, present and supernatural. They are part of a tradition stretching back millennia yet have a vision projecting into the next era.

New Zealand's best quilters, weavers, embroiderers, felters, dyers and creators of wearable art are a dedicated lot. They have to be — they work very much in isolation, are often misunderstood by those they quickly outclass, and most earn little from their work. Many can only hope, as one veteran practitioner puts it, to 'eke together a living'. Of the women — the majority of textile artists — some have chosen childlessness; others struggle to support a family as well as find time to create.

There are often no categories for the work these artists make, and few venues for exhibiting it. Where these opportunities exist, they can be expensive — I was told more than once that the cost to enter the Norsewear Art Award has become too high. Yet, as with academics who must publish or perish, textile artists must be seen to become known, and they need to publicly offer their work for comparison alongside that of their peers.

Whether they align themselves strongly with visual artists — something that seems to work best in smaller communities — or practise alone, many textile artists struggle to build a financial and artistic support base. Some become more business-oriented so they can keep going; many produce a 'bread and butter' line of small pieces that allows them to work on their 'real' art the rest of the time. For a few, however brilliant, producing one-off pieces is so labour-intensive — both physically and emotionally — and support so paltry, they burn out.

And while we have no intention of stepping into the craft/art debate when it comes to textiles, here is a statement from veteran stitcher Malcolm Harrison, inaugural recipient in 2004 of Creative New Zealand's craft and object art fellowship, that elegantly sums up the difference: 'Craft is where you take the parameters and work within them. Art is where the medium is stretched to breaking point and emotion is conjured up' (Malcolm Harrison, 2006).

Mieke Apps

IT WOULD BE EASY TO THINK MIEKE APPS TURNS OUT PRIZE QUILTS ALL THE TIME, SO MANY AWARDS HAS SHE WON. BUT THE FIRST NEW ZEALAND QUILTER TO WIN A MAJOR INTERNATIONAL AWARD FINDS THINGS DON'T ALWAYS HAPPEN ACCORDING TO PLAN — JUST ONE REASON WHY SHE MAKES ONLY TWO MAJOR QUILTS EACH YEAR.

RIGHT: Pacific Rhythm *combines Mieke's past as a weaver with her love of her adopted country.*

'm quite a slow worker,' Mieke says. 'To me, everything about a quilt has to work — the design, colours, stitching, technical details. When I hang a quilt I want not a ripple.'

A string of successes has followed that first award, in 1994, for *Requiem*. But Mieke's search for perfection has led her more than once to throw quilts into the bin in frustration. One of these was *Lux Victus*, the Dupion silk work that won an award at Quilt Expo V in the home of the French silk industry, Lyon. 'If my friend Barbara Bilyard had not literally pulled that quilt out of the rubbish bin, it would probably never have been finished.'

Mieke started out as a rug and tapestry weaver in the seventies, but arthritis in her hands put an end to that career in 1988. Work from this era is held in collections and public institutions, including the Dunedin Public Art Gallery. However, Mieke had always sewn, and when she organised a big arts festival exhibition in Putaruru in 1989, featuring pioneer art quilter Jo Cornwall, she began her quilting journey.

Colour is Mieke's greatest motivation — she won a Ciba-Geigy colour award as a weaver and now dyes all her own fabric, selling lengths from her Kerikeri home.

Mieke was born 70 years ago in Hoorn, an historic town in West Friesland, a northwestern region of the Netherlands, where boats left for the Indies and came back laden with spices

and cloth. She began life in a house full of colour, literature and music. Taught to knit as a five-year-old, she recalls making a doll's jacket in salmon pink, with a matching bonnet, embroidered with lazy daisies. Occupation by the Germans changed everything, bringing hardship and starvation to the people of the town. For some years, Mieke's only dolls were made of potatoes and matchsticks.

After the war, she received a sound tertiary education at an institution in Amsterdam. Its name translates as 'The Industrial School for Young Women', and it taught everything to do with textiles and applied arts. She learnt tailoring, sewing, embroidery, knitting, drawing and pattern-making. This education has stood Mieke in good stead, when it comes to drawing

RIGHT: Star Crossed *won an international award for Mieke Apps, pictured above in her Kerikeri studio.*

'I never fitted in the quilt world,' Mieke says. 'But when I came here, the painters treated me like an equal artist and not like a craftsperson.'

---

the large, flowing pieces she uses in her quilts. As a challenge to herself, in her latest quilt, *From The Inside* (left), she takes the internal cut from another spiral shape and works with just two colours.

Mieke left Holland in late 1955 and moved with her parents to Australia, where her father, Jacob Waterman, became a well-known painter. Mieke came to New Zealand in 1962 and married her husband Graeme in 1966. After he was made redundant, they left their Titirangi home and moved to Kerikeri, and although she misses the bush, which inspired more than one quilt, Mieke says coming to Kerikeri has been 'the very best thing'. The real bonus has been discovering a community of artists.

'I never fitted in the quilt world,' Mieke says. 'But when I came here, the painters treated me like an equal artist and not like a craftsperson.'

She has developed wall-mounted paint and fibre works that fit the required format for painters' exhibitions, as well as having solo shows. Meeting regularly with other artists in a workshop situation has given her a new way of designing her own work. 'They'll be drawing and I'll be relating ideas to fabric. It's a new phase for me.'

Star Crossed (page 13) was inspired by photos of coloured gases taken from the Space Probe, and won the Best Workmanship award at Quilt Expo VII in Strasbourg.

Another award-winner, *Pacific Rhythm* (page 11), goes back to her work as a weaver and combines stitch, design and weaving in an attempt to create a truly New Zealand quilt which includes trees and orange tones to create an impression of a volcanic lava flow.

Refusing to do commissions — making a chore out of what should be joyful and spontaneous — Mieke is happiest on her own and, while totally absorbed in her quilting, often works with little social contact for several months at a time. She has wide musical tastes, and plays classical baroque while she quilts, on a tiny stereo she bought for her backyard studio. For additional company, she has Jellybean, a tabby kitten that races her to the studio door each morning. ■

LEFT: From the Inside
uses two colours only,
including a spiral offcut from
another quilt.

Victoria Bell

THE IDEA FOR TEXTILE ARTIST VICTORIA BELL'S *PEACOCK FOUNTAIN* SCULPTURE CAME TO HER IN A MOMENT OF CLARITY. 'ALL OF A SUDDEN I SAW CLEARLY THAT, OF COURSE, THE NEXT THING TO DO WAS MAKE A VERY LARGE FOUNTAIN.'

Creating the four-metre-high work (right) was another matter entirely for the Canterbury artist, who is currently studying for a Master of Fine Arts at the Otago Polytechnic School of Art in Dunedin. 'Naiveté is a great thing,' Victoria says. 'I was hugely ambitious about what I wanted to achieve.'

The Peacock Fountain/Design No. 38 is Victoria's take on Christchurch's controversial Peacock Fountain, which was a bequest to the city from the Honourable John Peacock, a businessman, MP and early mayor of St Albans. The design chosen for the piece — first installed in 1911 near the Robert McDougall Art Gallery, restored at great cost and in lurid colour in 1996, and now situated in the entrance to the Christchurch Botanic Gardens — was number 38 in a catalogue of English fountains, rather than a proposed local design that cost more, but would have incorporated native flora and fauna.

The theme for Christchurch's Art &

Industry Urban Arts Biennial in 2004 — how the Asia Pacific region has influenced the cultural evolution of New Zealand — gave Victoria the chance to explore themes of Pacific identity from the point of view of someone who is neither Maori nor Pacific Islander, but is strongly connected to New Zealand's place in the Pacific Rim. Her version of the Peacock Fountain colourfully interpreted the original with a contemporary eye — in fabric.

'Swathed in textiles sweet and sour', she saw it as 'sculpture which had evolved from craft origins rather than a sculptural basis'. This was in keeping with her maternal family history, which is rich in aunts and great-aunts, collectors of precious fabrics and hoarders of a century's worth of threads, silks and hand-sewn wedding gowns — a past where distinctions between 'craft' and 'art' were irrelevant.

For a young artist more experienced in two-dimensional and textile-based arts, the shift to self-supporting work on this scale brought

Victoria Bell's fabric
interpretation of
Christchurch's controversial
Peacock Fountain
— 'swathed in textiles sweet
and sour'.

Trees from the **Dear Victoria** *installation, a collaboration between Victoria Bell and Victoria Edwards, at The Physics Room in Christchurch, which also included a deer's head.*

challenges of its own. An internal armature on which to hang her fountain was needed to retain the form, and although Victoria initially intended to construct it herself, she soon realised the scale of the work necessitated calling in specialist technical support. This took the form of an experienced sheetmetal worker, who constructed the fountain's infrastructure.

For its installation in Christchurch's Centre of Contemporary Art (CoCA), the elements had to be able to fit through a doorway and up stairs — which rather determined how things finally worked out.

Creating the Peacock Fountain eventually became a collaborative process for Victoria, as family, friends and fellow artists were invited

'Most of the elements on the fountain originate from flat cut-outs from my pattern drafts. They've become 3D by default, from the process of construction and the action of stuffing.'

to help hand-sew fabric elements onto the fountain's metal pieces. 'This was an amazing, humbling, gorgeous thing,' she says, 'to allow other hands to work on my work.'

The inclusive nature of its construction has continued with the exhibition of the Peacock Fountain. One comment in the visitors' book at the gallery reads, 'If I were a cat then I would hunt your dolphin and chase your pigeons before curling up for a nap on the top of your fountain'. A Japanese student wrote, 'Your art make me pop . . . happy. Thank you'.

Until she started making the fountain, Victoria had produced mostly soft sculpture artworks, grounded by a strong drawing practice. Her graduating work from Christchurch Polytechnic's School of Art and Design was a series of silk and satin, screenprinted and embroidered, pockets and panels. 'It looked like I was ready to go into the textile-printing field, although my interest lay in continuing to explore making one-off pieces that could wrap the body but resist becoming garments,' she says.

However, volume and dimension became more and more important — a total surprise to one who had always found the sculpture area at the Polytechnic 'so challenging — and all that wood!' Yet in spite of the move from textiles to sculpture, Victoria still conceives things in a two-dimensional way. 'Most of the elements on the fountain originate from flat cut-outs from my pattern drafts. They've become 3D by default, from the process of construction and the action of stuffing.

'Coincidentally,' Victoria says, 'after making the Peacock Fountain I received the Olivia Spencer Bower Award and I ended up living at the Arts Centre, in an apartment opposite the Botanic Gardens — looking directly at the original Peacock Fountain every day! Such is fate.' ■

Freda Brierley

FREDA BRIERLEY DRAWS WITH HER SEWING MACHINE. THE HUMAN
FIGURE IS HER SUBJECT, AND HER TECHNICAL ABILITY IN CAPTURING
LIGHT AND SHADE ALLOWS HER AS MUCH SCOPE AS SOMEONE DRAWING
WITH MORE CONVENTIONAL TOOLS.

 from ethereal everyman or woman figures, Freda has moved to portraits so individual you can almost hear their voices; and they invariably speak with a Scottish accent.

A reluctant immigrant who came to Devonport in 1982 when her husband transferred from the Royal Navy to the New Zealand Navy, Freda firmly believes that you must create from what you know — in her case, Dundee, Scotland, where she grew up. Using family photographs she has brought to life her own past, and referred to a broader social history as well.

The two figures shown on pages 22 and 23, from her 2005 Auckland Museum exhibit 'A Weavers' Tale', depict her Scottish grandmother Georgina — holding the shuttle — and her friend Nell, with thread dangling from her pocket and scissors in her hand. Made using machine embroidery and by drawing on linen, the finished works are an amalgam of photographs taken in the mill and research into what a weaver might have worn and had on her person. The project was one that involved Freda's father

— Georgina's son — shortly before his death, and Freda's mother, who had been a weaver in the jute mills as a girl and was a great source of information about factory life and the camaraderie of the women.

As a girl, Freda had wanted to go to art school. Instead, she became a nurse like her great-aunt, who was a missionary nurse in the Congo. From there Freda joined the Royal Navy as a Sister in Queen Alexandra's Nursing Service; all the time 'dabbling in art, taking the odd class, and entering exhibitions'. She finally got to art school, Whitecliffe in Auckland, in 1989 and has been making art ever since.

'I'm pretty much on my own — not many people do what I do,' Freda says. In spite of the 'very unexpected' honour of being awarded life membership to the North Shore Embroiderers' Guild, she now aligns herself not so much with traditional embroiderers but with artists

LEFT: **The Swimmer** *was selected for an international machine embroidery exhibition in France.*

'My first love is drawing and mark-making — it's always exciting and frequently frustrating. Using the human figure to convey a mood or situation will always be integral with my work.'

— painters and art quilters. 'My first love is drawing and mark-making — it's always exciting and frequently frustrating. Using the human figure to convey a mood or situation will always be integral with my work.'

An only child, Freda was taught embroidery by her mother — doilies, crinoline ladies and kitsets. It wasn't until she went to a creative embroidery class in Dundee, where there was not a kitset in sight, that she experienced an epiphany. Her first work was decorative, applied to traditionally embroidered objects such as hussifs and boxes. Then she started to draw pictures from her own history. 'It was much better than cross-stitch! I really like to draw — I used to draw a lot. Then I wasn't at all confident to paint. So I started to draw on my sewing machine to show it can be done.'

First exhibited at the National Association of Embroiderers' Guilds' 2002 exhibition at the New Zealand Academy of Fine Arts in Wellington, the work *Does Someone Know His Name?* featured a faceless child sitting on a mother's

Freda Brierley's Scottish grandmother Georgina *(right) and her friend* Nell *(left), weavers in Dundee's jute mills, featured in her exhibition 'A Weaver's Tale' at Auckland Museum in* 2005.

knee. 'Some people thought it was a morbid comment on dead children,' says Freda, 'those that never reached adulthood. But to tell you the truth this never entered my head.' Looking through the family album there was always the question, 'Who is this child? What is his name?' and her mother would say, 'I dinna ken'.

'I thought, does someone know his name or are we all doomed to be a forgotten face on an old brown picture?'

Freda says that for some time her work has been constantly looking backwards, ' . . . trying to hold on to things past. Maybe it is true when they say that you cannot know where you are going till you know where you've been,' she says.

Is it time for a change of focus perhaps? 'Well, maybe. What has changed, and is changing,' she says, 'is my attitude to the viewer. Whereas before I gave this little thought, I now find added excitement by trying to tease and deceive, by creating puzzles, by concealing and revealing the truth with gaps to be filled, making many interpretations possible'. ■

Gutsy — Susan Broad's lacy crocheted bowl.

Susan Broad

WHEN IT COMES TO MATERIALS FOR HER CROCHET SCULPTURES, SUSAN BROAD FINDS PIG INTESTINES MUCH EASIER TO MANIPULATE THAN SHEEP GUT.

wo creamy, vase-like structures first shown at the Creative Fibre exhibition in Wellington in 2005 had visitors guessing — until they read the catalogue notes. One was made of crocheted flax, the other, pig intestine. Both pieces sold.

A committed weaver for many years, Susan turned to crochet when she became frustrated that the only three-dimensional work she could make on her loom was tubular. 'Double-weave is too restrictive, it always comes out as a tube,' she says. 'Crochet has the ability to change shape.' Susan prefers the edge she can produce with crochet stitches to a knitted shape; plastic household objects wrapped in tinfoil are used to hold the floppy pig intestine shape while it dries.

Susan makes a point of using recycled materials in almost everything she crafts, whether it's jewellery or sculpture. This includes unwinding armatures for their copper wire — a time-intensive procedure that's more important for its environmental consequences than any savings in cost — and crocheting plastic bags. One of her inspirations is UK queen of recycled textiles, Eyv Saunders, who was brought to New Zealand by the British Council in 2003 for workshops in association with the touring 'Recycled' exhibition.

A spinner since the age of eighteen, when she fled Auckland for Te Anau and the tourist hotel scene and had to find something to do during winter lay-offs, Susan has even tried

Vase crafted from pig intestine.

define the direction she wanted to take.

Susan and her husband raised their family in Blenheim before moving to Dunedin — 'the best city in New Zealand!' — in 2004 where the art scene — especially textile art — is lively, with both the university and polytechnic faculties involved. Susan is heartened that more and more textiles, including those using three dimensions, are being selected for the annual Cleveland Art Awards. In addition, jewellery — including much that is alternative — has been given a big boost with Cleveland's Oceana Gold award, sponsored by the goldmining company of the same name.

It was while still at school that Susan first wove on a couple of sticks, without realising what she was doing. In the sixth form, she watched a new arrival being given a two-way loom to play with while the rest of the art class continued to paint. 'I thought, how do I get one of those? I would go in at playtime and lunchtime to use it.' Later, when she was at home after her children were born, her husband gave her a 24-inch, rigid-heddle loom on which she made 'the bizarrest of massive blankets, woven in strips, mostly of my own lumpy handspun yarns.'

With her loom packed in a corner while renovations are carried out, Susan has been increasingly feeling the need to get back to weaving. 'The ideas are bubbling . . . I need to get it out and work on something I'm thinking of which will probably have a felted finish.

'You go full circle and loop back,' she says. 'I'm not technique-based — it's good to have a bunch of skills, then you can visualise the end product and decide which skill to use.' ■

spinning plastic bags, shredding them first. The plastic rubbish bag medallion that adorns her garden fence could be wrought iron, but it's not and it won't rust. She is keen to make freestanding garden sculptures using armatures, an idea that is strengthened each time she sees a supermarket car park littered with plastic bags.

Susan likes to trick viewers with double-takes. Her bread-and-butter line of crocheted, copper wire necklaces look truly lace-like and, because they are quick to make, can be reasonably priced. A 2005 workshop in Nelson with found-object artist Keith Lo Bue gave her an insight into metal. Silversmithing classes in Dunedin also refined her use of metals and helped her

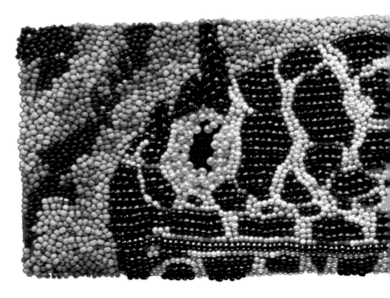

Blue Iguana *is one of Rebecca Brown Thompson's 'beaded heirlooms'.*

Rebecca Brown Thompson

WHEN THE WEATHER IS GOOD, REBECCA BROWN THOMPSON IS OUTSIDE SKETCHING IN THE WILD. WHEN IT GETS COLDER, SHE CREATES EXQUISITE BEADED WORK, BASED LARGELY ON WHAT SHE HAS OBSERVED IN NATURE.

a scientific illustrator, Rebecca was born in Columbus, Indiana, but now lives in Christchurch. She has a degree in horticulture from Purdue University, plus an enduring interest in overlooked, rare and unusual plants from all over the world, many of which appear in her beading as well as her nature drawings.

She first came across beading at a Mountain Man Rendezvous in Montana, USA. At the craft gathering's bead booth, she saw beautiful bead embroidery on Cree Indian clothing. 'I thought, that's kind of cool, I could do that. I never knew seed beads even existed before that.'

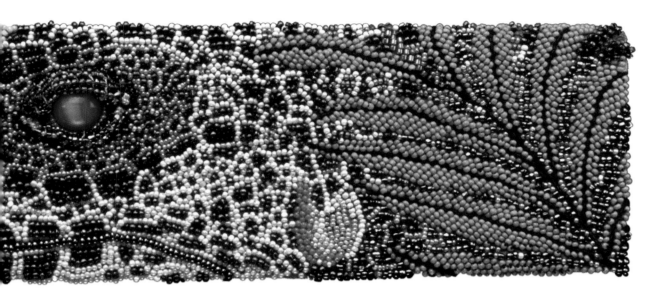

She discovered that the native American people did not bead with glass beads until Europeans arrived, bringing beads as gifts and barter. Their early designs were based on European fabrics — flowers and geometric quill work patterns. Now they work in what has since become their tradition, using their own motifs — which vary from tribe to tribe — while a new generation of non-native beaders follow quite different paths.

Looking for a teacher, Rebecca says she was fortunate to be living in Idaho, a part of the Pacific Northwest region that is a mecca for beaders and glass work. The person she found, Sharon Bateman, has since become her best friend and they continue to work together, one in Christchurch, New Zealand, the other in Idaho, USA.

Rebecca's basic ingredients are mostly from the Czech Republic and Japan; she also crafts silver clasps and does some enamelling when the design calls for it.

'Beading seems to be a skill that is enjoyed across many cultures. One thing about the beads is that they are glass and pretty much made the same way they were hundreds of years ago, so not only am I working directly with history as far as material goes, but the quality actually has got better as well as the techniques.'

Although a science illustrator throughout her working life, Rebecca says it took her a while to get her head around the three-dimensional nature of beading, but she finds she can now do things with beads she would never attempt to draw. 'It's a different mindset. Science illustrating has to be so exact. With the beads, they dictate what's going to happen. Plus they're tactile, and I love tactile!'

As well as one-off showpieces of wearable art, Rebecca works on commission to produce personal pieces, within a client's budget, specialising in sculptured relief work. Most of her commissions come through her website: 'Mainly American clientele as my designs seem to suit that market more.' Most pieces take over 200 hours of work — and that is just the beading, without considering design and finishing.

Function is important: 'It needs to have a reason to be made'. So there are woven, off-loom or bead-embroidered collars with titles such as *Leaf Lei, The Garden of Eden, Portuguese Man-o-War* and *Liverwort Delite*, with the occasional bag, bracelet and headpiece.

For eighteen years, Rebecca has been a member and vice-president of the international Guild of Natural Science Illustrators, which was set up in the 1970s by a group of scientific illustrators at the Smithsonian Institution. She still attends conferences in the US whenever possible to keep up to date with techniques. She is so far the only New Zealander in the guild, although there are several Australians.

As well as unusual, rare and endangered plants, her preferred botanical subjects include those with a medicinal use. Whenever possible, she tries to draw plants in the field, in their natural environment, and she especially appreciates New Zealand natives — native orchids are in her sights for the 2006 spring, as well as alpine plants.

Rebecca and her husband came to New Zealand for the lifestyle it offered them and their 19-year-old son, and now hold dual citizenship. Since arriving in 1999, she has thrown herself into the craft-artist scene in Christchurch.

'It has been a joy living in a city that not only loves its beautiful gardens but is also art orientated as well, not to mention the high concentration of excellent craft artists in every field of craftwork, whose expertise I can draw on.'

BELOW: Portuguese Man-o-War *is a beaded collar inspired by the deadly jellyfish.*

'My goal is to make heirloom pieces. You can't buy many things anymore that you would truly call heirloom, items you would pass on to your children.'

Liverwort Delite
magnifies the beauty of a humble botanical plant.

Her beadwork is featured in shows and magazines such as *Bead and Button* and she has participated in numerous juried shows in the US. *Blue Iguana* (page 26) is one of seven projects featured in an instructional book on advanced three-dimensional beading that Rebecca is publishing in 2006.

Earlier in the year, Rebecca was one of 35 international artists whose work was exhibited at LAX airport as part of 'Art 2 Wear', mounted jointly by the City of Los Angeles Department of Cultural Affairs and Los Angeles World Airports. One of their most popular exhibits to date, it just proves, Rebecca says, that people really respond to craft art.

'My goal is to make heirloom pieces. You can't buy many things anymore that you would truly call heirloom, items you would pass on to your children — production pieces just don't hold the same value. So I have put myself in this very small niche market partly because I want to, and partly because that is a market I know. Even though I am not commercial by any means, I do not consider beading a hobby but rather a mission, to set high standards in this art form.

'I do these elaborate pieces of beading because I want them to be special. They are not just beadwork, but works of art.' ∎

RIGHT: **The Brainchild of the Clewless,** *which stands nearly a metre tall, combines the human brain and symbols of the labyrinth with an intricately knitted child's dress.*

Andrea Chandler

A SENSE OF MELANCHOLY — FOR THE LOSS OF ANCIENT KNOWLEDGE AND HANDCRAFT SKILLS PASSED DOWN THROUGH GENERATIONS — PERVADES ANDREA CHANDLER'S TEXTILE-BASED WORK. HER OWN HAPPY CHILDHOOD MEMORIES ONLY ADD TO HER AWARENESS OF WHAT TODAY'S GENERATION IS LOSING.

 ndrea is conscious of the rapid disappearance of the sorts of things she learned as a child in constructive play. 'Mine was a really happy childhood and I always seemed to have some sort of creative project on the go,' the Nelson artist says. 'I remember the great sense of achievement and pleasure I got from these activities. In fact, many of the techniques I use now as part of my art practice are those learnt at quite an early age from my mother.'

The *Brainchild of the Clewless* and *Warhead* works (page 31 and 32) initially arose from Andrea's sense of awe at the beautiful form of the brain, and the potential we each have as a result of this complex structure.

'The *Warhead* works,' she says, 'are essentially acts of personal protest. They comment on

'I remember the great sense of achievement and pleasure I got from these activities. In fact, many of the techniques I use now as part of my art practice are those learnt at quite an early age from my mother.'

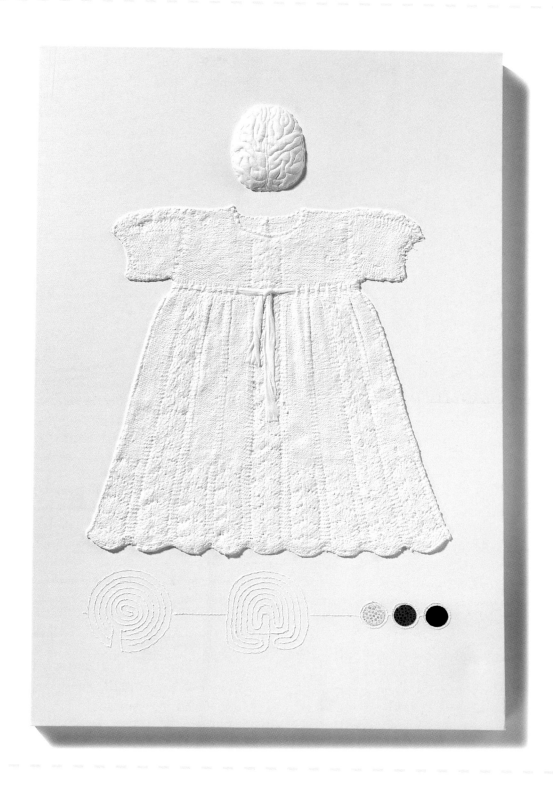

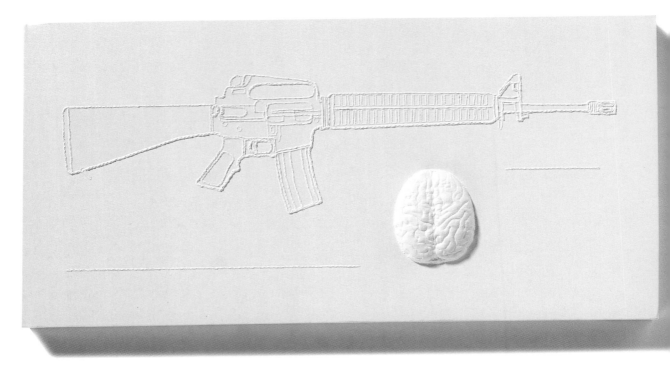

Warhead *is a protest against humankind's obsession with the tools of aggression. At 760mm wide, the work is almost the same size as the gun it represents.*

humankind's obsession with devising and refining the tools of aggression. From the club and spear of ancient times, we have steadily "progressed" to the present high-tech world of escalating militarism. Although it is now veneered in state-of-the-art sophistication, the innate barbarism of our species remains persistent.'

In some ways Andrea sees herself as an 'unrepentant nostalgic'. In appreciation of handcraft skills practised by a generation now gone, she often feels compelled to 'rescue' items such as the hand-knitted baby dress used in

Brainchild of the Clewless. The spelling of clewless is a very old one relating to the labyrinth symbols used in this work. The original meaning of clew was a ball of yarn — something Andrea thinks of as the 'thread of knowledge' — that was wound up to help guide one out of a maze.

She relishes the opportunity to learn a new skill if this is what is needed to fully realise her ideas. When the 'furrows and grooves' of the brain motif called for quilting, which was new to her, she started stitching the sandwich of light cotton, dacron and calico by hand, but had to find an alternative because it was taking

'I'm most confident when working with textiles,' she says. 'I constantly find myself drawn back to the ritual, methodical, almost meditative aspect of these processes.'

too long. In keeping with her respect for the old ways — Andrea is deliberately low-tech in her own practice — she used her 1922 treadle sewing machine to quilt the brains, which were then padded and sewn onto the canvas before being sealed with acrylic.

Committing herself to future exhibitions gives Andrea the impetus to concentrate on developing an idea 'without being bound by the constraints of saleability', which is a consideration when crafting her more decorative works such as jewellery and crocheted copper bags. 'An exhibition is an opportunity for me to develop a body of work that explores a particular theme, or voices a current social or environmental concern,' she says. 'I am interested in exploring the gently subversive potential of handcraft techniques when applied to themes outside the traditional arena of domesticity and decoration.'

A graduate of Wellington Polytechnic's clothing and textile design course during the 1980s, Andrea completed a Diploma in Visual Arts (Sculpture) at Nelson Polytechnic a decade later and now combines skills from both areas in her work. She is more than competent with a crochet hook, having worked on a large scale

with copper wire at two of the Mac's Sculpture Symposia run by the Nelson Arts Festival, armed with just a crochet hook and her ear muffs. Her large but delicate copper *Diatom Shield* (2002) and *Sea Keepers* (2003), based on minute sea creatures, were competing with 'big bloke stuff', another example of the subversion offered by textile techniques.

Andrea was one of the sculptors invited to take part in the Co-incidence Project, a Creative New Zealand-funded, site-specific sculpture symposium at Pakawau, on the eastern shores of Golden Bay, over New Year 2003. The ideas she explored in this project, when she used rugmaking techniques to hook plastic bags into synthetic weed mat, later led to her entry in the touring exhibition 'Handycrafts: At Home with Textiles'.

'I'm most confident when working with textiles,' she says. 'I constantly find myself drawn back to the ritual, methodical, almost meditative aspect of these processes.' ■

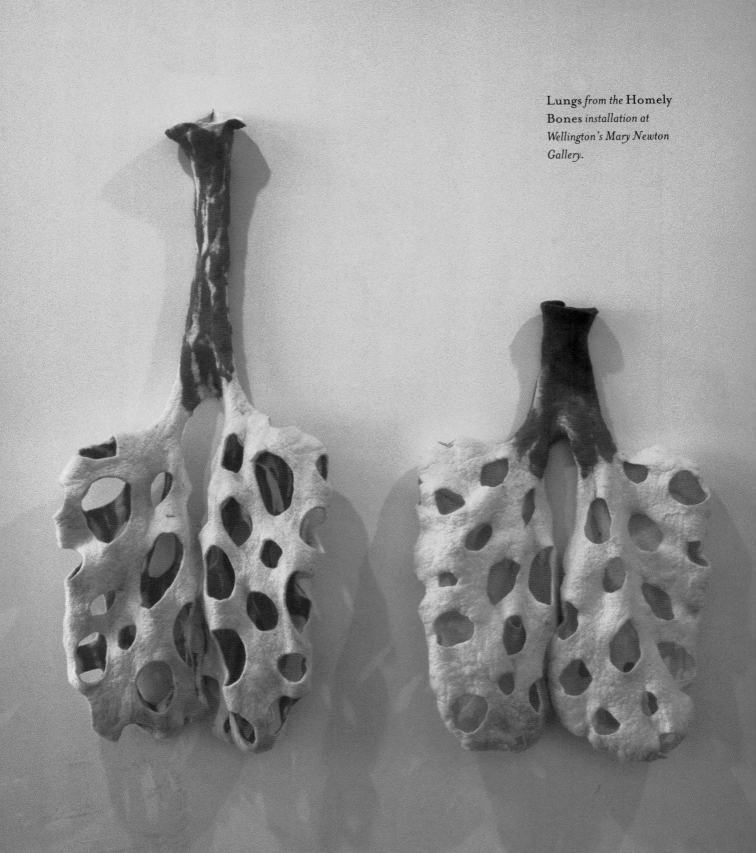

Lungs *from the* Homely
Bones *installation at
Wellington's Mary Newton
Gallery.*

Andrea du Chatenier

FABRICATING THINGS WAS ALWAYS IMPORTANT IN ANDREA DU CHATENIER'S FAMILY, SO MOVING FROM AUCKLAND TO A CITY WITH AN ABUNDANCE OF TEXTILES WAS BOUND TO RESULT IN NEW FIBRE WORKS.

andrea du Chatenier's art has touched on textiles before, but it is only since she settled into life in Wanganui that she has developed her fondness for natural fibre. Her latest works are constructed of thick handmade felt, a result of wool being so freely available in the region. The red, white and black works that make up *Homely Bones* (opposite) and *Autopsy* (page 36) were exhibited at the Mary Newton Gallery in Wellington in 2005, and key works from *Homely Bones* are now in The Dowse collection in Lower Hutt.

Although she has been a lecturer in art and design for ten years, Andrea began with a craft design course at Waikato Polytechnic before starting her fine arts degree at Elam, and also has a Masters from RMIT in Melbourne. She taught at Unitec in Auckland before becoming artist-in-residence at the Sarjeant Gallery's Tylee Cottage in 2003, and she now lectures to fine art students at Quay School of the Arts in Wanganui.

'Coming here gave me access to the skills of people around about,' she says. 'There's an emphasis on textiles here, with the fashion school, spinners and weavers everywhere, and other guilds. There are woolshops, second-hand shops, fantastic op-shops and recycled textiles.' A huge recycle mart is just a block away from where Andrea lives with her partner Anthony Davies, who is also an artist, and their Dalmatians, Tag and Ruby.

Materials have always been an important part of Andrea's work. 'I like the way materials have particular associations for people, and that by manipulating and transforming materials I can play with these meanings,' she says. 'At the moment I am really enjoying using felt because of its associations with children's toys and with a kind of homely handcraftiness. There's an earnestness about natural fibres that harks back to the 1970s, when wearing homespun clothes and making ceramics were part of a back-to-nature dream. Part of that dream still lingers but now we view its simplicity with a little more irony. The forms I make from felt have a playfulness about them, but the irony of our

'The forms I make from felt have a playfulness about them but the irony of our desire for an authentic naturalness is also there.'

desire for an authentic naturalness is also there.'

Andrea often uses animals in her works to explore ideas of human relationships and foibles in what writer Tessa Laird has called 'inter-species drag'. She uses the paradoxical qualities of what we find appealing (or not) in creatures like dogs and monkeys as a way of looking at ourselves. The Dowse has two PVC animal suits in their collection — *Horse* and *Monkey* — which were first exhibited as part of the exhibition 'Henry Sarjeant's Fine Art Department Store' at the Sarjeant Gallery, following Andrea's residency at the Tylee Cottage.

The 'Origin Pod' range — presumably sold at Sarjeant's department store — is 'a range of luggage for a new world order that presumes a world where the current human/animal hierarchies are undone'. It includes human hair bags, bone bags and nest hats. Andrea says the animal suits are 'bondage gear, created to allow humans the opportunity to practise playing the submissive role in the relationship'. The label comes from cropping the advertising slogan

LEFT: *Autopsy, a line-up of felted monkey and human interchangeable body parts, plays on the irony of soft textiles with a gruesome subject.*

' . . . bondage gear, created to allow humans the opportunity to practise playing the submissive role in the relationship.'

Canary from
Homely Bones.

'Original Production' from the Levi Strauss company.

Reanimation of the Dispossessed was based on animals from the Samuel Drew Collection at the Whanganui Regional Museum, which includes a range of rare and extinct animals such as the Tasmanian tiger, a creature that met the same end as our huia, hunted to extinction by collectors.

Andrea's early works often used inflatable shapes such as a silver polyethylene foil tree. Some of her early animals are now reappearing in felt, such as the monkey in *Autopsy* (page 36). Looking for someone to teach her felting, Andrea found Raewyn Penrose of Te Aroha and attended one of her workshops, taking along her mother, who shares her pleasure in 'the skill of doing things'. Felting is very quick and very easy, Andrea says. 'I'm not a knitter or a crocheter — that takes too much time.'

Andrea is continuing to work in felt, and developing the idea of regeneration. Her next exhibition is scheduled for May 2007 at the Mary Newton Gallery. ■

A view of the Homely
Bones installation at
Mary Newton Gallery.

Lindy Chinnery

The first time Lindy Chinnery entered a Creative Fibre competition she won both the novice and the supreme fashion awards. While she won't be able to pull off the double again, she has continued to feature in the annual Creative Fibre and biennial Professional Weavers' Network of New Zealand selections. In addition, she now has a charming shop in the little Otago town of Lawrence.

Lawrence — best known for the discovery of gold in nearby Gabriel's Gully — has become a welcome stop on the road from Dunedin to the Lakes, especially now it has half a dozen cafes in its once-deserted main street. Since 2004, Lawrence has also had a Textile Emporium in the old Athenaeum Library, which dates from 1865. The space has been beautifully refurbished to show off richly hued weaving, knitting, embroidery, felting and yarns on one side, and owner Lindy Chinnery's loom on the other.

Lindy was working from a studio at home on the block she and her partner bought fourteen years ago — at just under a hectare, somewhere to keep a few pet sheep and grow hazelnut trees — when she heard the shop was up for lease. As well as raising the profile of regional textile artists, the Emporium enables her to experiment with

One of Lindy Chinnery's collapsed weave scarves.

'No matter what we do to preserve our creations,' she says,
'nature will eventually reclaim what is rightfully hers.'

her own work in a way that was not possible when she was selling it through other shops around the South Island.

'It's difficult to get good outlets that show your work well,' she says. 'And when your work is selling in other places you don't get the feedback. It's not just a matter of working with what comes out of the dyepot, or what's selling at the moment, you can be a lot more experimental — and you get feedback. People react to what you're doing. It's great to have contact with the public.'

Sydney-born Lindy learnt the fundamentals of weaving after her mother died, leaving Lindy her spinning wheel. Needing to relearn the skill of spinning she went to tutor Ailsa Trainor, saw a loom, fell in love and ended up fitting in workshops around her day job. When she and her Kiwi partner decided the time was right to come back to New Zealand, they started taking Sunday drives south from Christchurch, looking for rural properties. That was fourteen years ago.

Lindy indulges her love of rich, lush colour and texture when she designs her individual fabrics. Inspired by Persian carpets and Indian and Moroccan textiles, she dyes her own yarns to capture the same richness and depth of colour. 'Silk and wool are so beautiful to dye but I also love chenille, mohair and possum-fur yarns.'

She has also discovered alpaca, which dyes equally well. 'It's very light and soft. I love trying new yarns — it keeps the excitement in the weaving.'

Texture is equally important, and Lindy often achieves three-dimensional effects by combining different yarns, some that felt and some that pucker, producing a variation in tension that adds interest. 'In my weaving I'm not interested in traditional weaves, but in colour and textural effects,' she says.

Lindy also weaves garments using the yarns of Alexandra-based company Touch Yarns, for in-store displays and trade shows in the US, UK and Australia, as well as the company's own premises overlooking the Clutha River.

Like their earlier themed shows, the Professional Weavers' Network's exhibition 'Black and White — A Journey Through Contrasts', which toured nationally in 2004, offered the chance to go beyond what can be worn. Lindy had been reading a newspaper item about how the jungle encroaches, and thinking about how we try to tame nature. 'If we don't maintain it, it will devour us,' she says. This led to her *hi-fibre diet* (opposite) — four wraps on miniature torsos, showing the predations of nature uncontrolled, in this case moths chomping on wool and feathers. 'No matter what we do to preserve our creations,' she says, 'nature will eventually reclaim what is rightfully hers.' ∎

hi-fibre diet *is Lindy Chinnery's ironic and miniature look at that arch-enemy of all who work in wool — moths.*

Vita Cochran's Zen-inspired **Shikaku** *bag is made from recycled men's suiting.*

A small purse to match the Shikaku *bag.*

Vita Cochran

RECYCLING IS IN THE GENES FOR
VITA COCHRAN — SHE SEEMS TO
HAVE INHERITED HER GRANDMOTHER
FLORA'S PENCHANT FOR TURNING
OVERLOOKED AND UNDERVALUED
THINGS INTO TREASURES. BUT THE
DUNEDIN DESIGNER—MAKER REVIVES
OLD TECHNIQUES AND REUSES ZIPS,
BUTTONS AND BUCKLES WITH MORE
PANACHE THAN ANYONE ELSE IN THE
COUNTRY.

growing up in Wellington, Vita was surrounded by family members who all did something crafty — mother, sister, aunts and cousins (boys included) who knitted and did canvas work, making up their own patterns, and a 'creative whirlwind' of a grandmother whose skills with a rug hook are carried on by Vita today. She was commissioned to make a rag rug for Bilbo Baggins' study for the *Lord of the Rings* trilogy, and has taught workshops in the craft, most recently at Gisborne Winter School in 2004, five months after her son Otto was born.

Vita is best known for her striking handbags, embellished with felt flowers or decorated with buttons and zips, which are held in collections at Te Papa Tongarewa and The Dowse. She feels

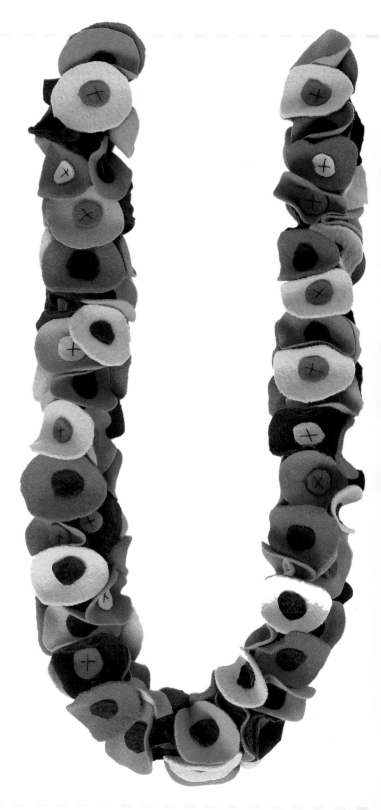

There are many small decisions that go into the creation of each item, and I love this making process and wouldn't swap it for anything.'

slightly uncomfortable with the textile artist label, preferring to call herself a 'designer—maker'.

'My practice sits between art and business models,' she says. 'On one hand I don't make one-off pieces, I make small runs of each design. On the other hand, it's important to me that I do the making myself, rather than hand designs over to an outworker. There are many small decisions that go into the creation of each item, and I love this making process and wouldn't swap it for anything.'

Vita has concentrated on entirely handmade versions of three or four designs each season, working in collaboration from 2001 to 2005 with Auckland designer Marilyn Sainty, now retired. One product of their collaboration, called the *Vita* dress, appears in Te Papa Tongarewa's recent *Icons* publication. Felt flowers on coats and skirts were followed by bags with snaking zips, shimmering fields of buttons and an array of *faux-naïve* felt illustrations. They are lovingly made in Vita's workroom at home, and sold in shops from Invercargill to Melbourne. Each item is unique: 'You're never going to get two the same.'

Four of Vita's handbags toured the country as part of the 'Handycrafts: At Home with Textiles' exhibition, curated by Nelson designer

Winter 2006's Petal scarf *(opposite) is like a 'warm woollen lei'. It matches the petal cuff (above).*

and lecturer Rose Griffen. Vita's work has also been seen in the exhibitions 'Flaunt' at Auckland Art Gallery and 'Wild Design' at Te Papa, and shown at the Bombay Sapphire Design Room as part of Air New Zealand Fashion Week in 2004.

Vita has continued to collect colourful vintage buttons and art deco buckles, offered in 2006 in bracelet form. And for Winter 2006 she made a Petal scarf (opposite) of wool felt discs — 'like a warm, woollen lei' — and the Shikaku bag (page 44), a square of folded and quilted cloth inspired by the Zen aesthetic of *wabi* or elegant poverty of materials. It also has resonances of Depression-era clothing and domestic linens for Vita, who collects sacking aprons from the period.

There wasn't much time left over for textiles while Vita was completing her academic studies, culminating in 1999 with a Master of Arts (First Class Honours) in Art History, from the University of Auckland. Following her dissertation on artist Rita Angus and her acts

of painterly 'self-fashioning', Vita curated a touring exhibition of the artist's self-portraits.

After moving south to Dunedin for her partner's job, Vita was able to devote all her time to making things. 'I was tired of spending whole days in front of a computer screen,' she says. 'Making was always something I loved and knew I would do. Living here gave me space to do it.'

Much of her fabric and haberdashery comes from local op-shops, including one where the manager closes early on days when she wants to go muttonbirding. Op-shopping is a weekly ritual too for Otto, now two years old, who can spend half an hour choosing a ten-cent toy.

Vita's 400-strong collection of handmade tea cosies — 100 of which went on show at The Dowse in Rosemary McLeod's 'Thrift and Fantasy' exhibition — is displayed in the downstairs entry of the classic sixties house she shares with Otto and his dad Justin Paton, writer, critic and curator of contemporary art at Dunedin Public Art Gallery. For one who cares so passionately for things of an earlier era, the glass-fronted house overlooking Woodhaugh Gardens is the perfect place to live.

While awaiting the birth of another baby, due in August 2006, Vita was appliquéing hessian handbags and preparing to embroider T-shirts for summer. This is something she has done before, and she likes the idea of hand-embellishing a utility garment. This was also the year for a very special contribution to her sister's wedding — hundreds of subtly coloured silk organza, velvet and felt flowers to embellish the gown, and cover a matching shoulder cape. 'I only have one sister, so this was a chance to go into decorative overdrive!' ■

Cheryl Comfort

Exploring the shades of black is an ongoing adventure for quilter Cheryl Comfort, who is inspired by the interplay of matt and sheen in artist Ralph Hotere's paintings.

a challenge to make a work that was 'uniquely New Zealand', for an American exhibition, led Cheryl Comfort down the dark path. 'Mountains and things were not me,' she says, 'so I started thinking about what else makes New Zealand unique. Though I never did make a quilt for the challenge, I decided to explore working with black, the national colour.

'People have asked if I'm depressed using that black,' she laughs. 'I really don't think so, I just love the way light reacts on black, especially when it's stitched and creates subtle shadows.'

Somewhere along the way she sold off her conventional patchwork fabric, the sort that fitted someone else's idea of what a quilt should be. 'It was pretty but it was not me,' she says. 'I like traditional quilts but they don't come out of me; I've only ever made a few traditional quilts before I started designing my own. It's the designing that's as satisfying, if not more so, than making, for me.'

The daughter of an embroiderer and a painter who can turn his hand to anything,

Cheryl has always lived in Christchurch, apart from a brief stint in Wellington, where she really started quilting. She has attended a variety of classes to give her a range of skills she can call on to create the effects she wants to achieve.

Returning to favourite gallery exhibitions and analysing why things work is a favourite pursuit. A Hotere exhibition in Dunedin some years ago and a more recent one at the Christchurch Art Gallery — where Cheryl is secretary to the Friends of the Gallery organisation — had a big impact on her. 'I went back and back,' she says. 'I love the way the gloss and matt surfaces change with the light as you move across in front of the painting.' There can be many sources of inspiration — the patterns created with overlapping metal rods used in a garment at a 'Japonism in Fashion' exhibition at Christchurch Art Gallery had her working on incorporating more metal in a quilt.

Many of her later quilts have followed the theme of black on black, some using a traditional patchwork block such as Pinwheel and closely covering the surface with free form quilting,

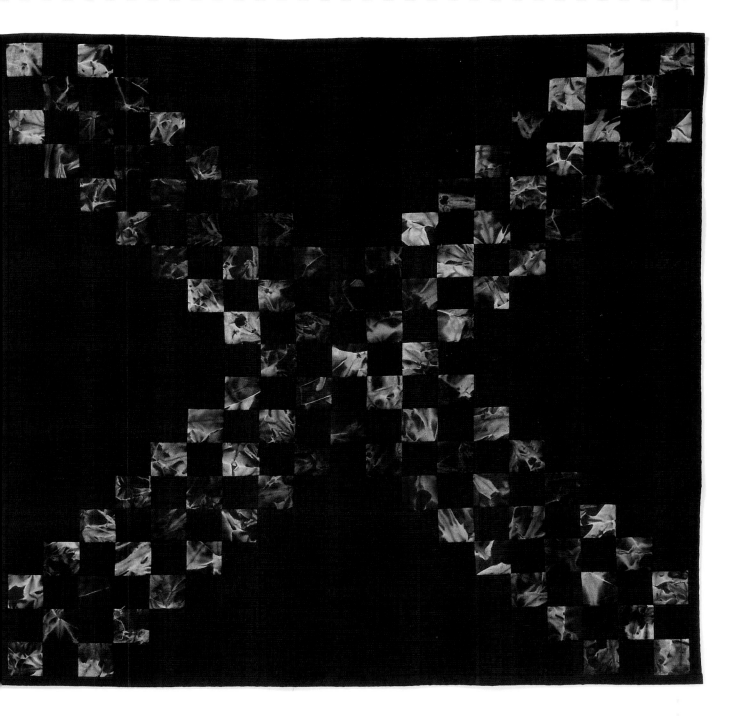

Absence and Existence IV *is one of a series based on the X-cross.*

where the direction is controlled by the quilter. Cheryl does a lot of machine-quilting, and says she loves the feel and texture of heavily quilted fabric. A black batting is essential in case white fibres 'beard' their way through to the surface.

She is continuing to explore the use of traditional patterns with non-traditional treatments, and is not afraid to use non-traditional materials in her quilts. Many of her works over the years have incorporated unusual synthetic fabrics; others in the *Absence and Existence* series include black hessian and copper shim (thin copper sheeting). 'I use whatever materials I need to get the look I'm after.'

Cheryl spends 'longer in the thinking than the making' and seizes any small opportunity for concentrated bursts of stitching. Since the birth of her daughter Ruby in late 2005, the chance to get out to her backyard studio has become increasingly rare, though four-year-old Ben is happy to play with pieces of fabric when his mother wants to sew.

Cheryl sees her quilts as divided into two sorts — those with something to say and those where she is just playing with design for the sheer pleasure of it. The *Absence and Existence* series,

Identity *hints at Maori cloaks.*

'can be pretty chaotic,' she says.

She buys black cloth in quantity from a Christchurch fabric store and often uses the discharge method (where a chemical takes out the black) to create an interesting pattern, such as in *Absence and Existence IV* (page 49), to mix with straight black. Or the top layer may be slashed to reveal another view, as in *Absence and Existence V*.

Cheryl is also fascinated by the effects of natural events on fabric — when a wired-together artwork started to show the effects of rust, she began thinking about the beauty of decomposition. A chance remark by a tutor about 'roasted teabags' had her experimenting in her own oven with a bolt of calico and the cheapest teabags she could find. The result of those two detours is *Unfinished Business*, a triptych about the layers of conflict that continue generation after generation. It includes cut-back layers, dangling threads and a slender horizontal panel of recycled wire, knitted by her friend Chris Tait.

Subtlety is important. The parchment look of *Unfinished Business* hints at something Middle Eastern; *Identity*, with its slightly padded squares and dangling red threads, has the look of a Maori cloak. There is also a reference in this work to the William Sutton memorial exhibition at Christchurch's Centre of Contemporary Art (CoCA), where the sight of the reverse of a tapestry by Kate Wells, complete with loose ends, especially appealed.

There's plenty more to explore yet, Cheryl says. 'I'm keen to do more mark-making, doodles almost, pencil on calico — something you know a real person has done. Of course it will be stitched — I couldn't give that up!' ∎

for example, looked at people's different lives and experiences. She was also intrigued that an 'X' can express an absence — as in a school roll — and someone's existence, as in a rudimentary signature. By contrast, in *Spinning in Silence* she was simply enjoying using different black fabrics to create the design. 'While I was trying to create a peaceful quilt, there's nothing especially deep and meaningful behind this one.'

In a number of recent works she has tried to instil a sense of quietness and stillness. 'I think it's a reaction to a busy life and house which, as everyone who's lived with pre-schoolers knows,

Jane Coughlan

ZANY, CRAZY, COLOURFUL —
JANE COUGHLAN'S LIFE IS AS
FULL-ON AS HER WILD AND
WACKY FABRIC CREATIONS.

a textile artist best known for
her cloth dolls, Jane Coughlan
bubbles over with ideas, most of
them multicoloured and three-
dimensional. One invariably spawns another, so
her characters have houses, cars and their own
dolls, a textural delight of hot pink, orange, red
and purple creations in yarn, cloth and fur that
raise a smile from the most serious viewers.

Based in Albany, just north of Auckland,
Jane teaches workshops, sells her patterns in
shops and over the internet, and regularly travels
to places like Houston's International Quilt
Market. She has designed a range of fabric for
the American market and was the guest exhibitor
at Expo Magic in the French city of Lyon in
2006.

Jane makes the most of every opportunity,
but only adds new skills to her repertoire when
they are needed for something specific — a six-
week course on welding, for example, enabled
her to make a falling angel weathervane for her
roof. Knowing how to weld, she says, is just like
knowing how to cook or sew.

Growing up in a family where everybody did

RIGHT: *Jane Coughlan's
hand stitched wool* Chick,
chick, chick, chick
*quilt takes a playful look at
the cheeky native pukeko.*

'You've got to be encouraging yet persuasive. People who make my designs want relaxation, not sweat and blood. It's got to be fun.'

something crafty — her mum was an art teacher, weaver, dressmaker and sculptor; her dad made furniture; her granny baked, gardened and sewed dolls' clothes for her — how could Jane not be creative?

Along with making her own clothes from a young age, Jane has amassed an 'extraordinary' collection of fabric and trims which she uses to create her own wardrobe. When her children were young she took up making bolsters (complete with stars and tassels) then soft sculpture, huge flowers, Christmas puddings and toothbrush draught-stoppers. She embarked on her first patchwork project when a friend wanted a draught-stopper for her house — a precision-pieced nightmare, especially in corduroy — then began teaching how to make them at night school.

Then, in 1993, the Wonder Woman of the cloth-doll world, Elinor Peace Bailey, visited New Zealand — and liberated Jane's 'doll within'. 'This extraordinary woman made it quite clear to me that making playful things was a valid pastime,' says Jane. The resulting *Red Hot Rag Dolls* led her on lively travels all over Australia and the US, journeys that continue as she develops new fabric creations.

It hasn't all been plain sailing for this passionate patchworker. Selling into a niche global market has been full of trials and tribulations, including freight hassles, customs problems and foreign tax dramas. The falling US dollar has also made dealing with the biggest craft market in the world a frustrating game.

The internet, however, has been fantastic, she says. 'It really serves niche markets like ours, those an inch wide and a mile deep.' She couldn't teach in person all over the world, but teaching online enables people to access her classes from all sorts of far-flung corners of the world. She has had students from places as widespread as Norfolk Island, the Seychelles, Alaska and Jamaica, many of whom would never have had access to mainstream craft classes.

Her early *Beach Babe* dolls have remained popular, but *Pippi's House* is her personal favourite. The stitch-your-own doll's house works very well for what Jane — a 'suppressed architect' herself and now the mother of an architecture student — calls the 'grandma' market (those young grans who want to make cute things for their grandbabies). 'It's a playful thing they make to celebrate their joy in their grandchildren,' she says. 'The kids often contribute, choosing buttons and colours, favourite fabrics and trims; it becomes a

collaborative project between grandmother and grandchild.'

After a few years focusing on family, successfully supporting son Chris' recovery from a head injury and daughter Anna through high school, Jane is getting back into her own career, starting with a communications degree at Massey University. 'My writing has always stood me in good stead,' she says. 'You've got to be encouraging yet persuasive. People who make my designs want relaxation, not sweat and blood. It's got to be fun.'

And she's getting back into quilting again. 'I'm lucky, really — I seem to have opportunities coming out my ears.' You can bet she's making the multicoloured most of them too. ■

The Nobodies
— 'a Polynesian bloke in a lavalava and a ditzy girl in high heels'.

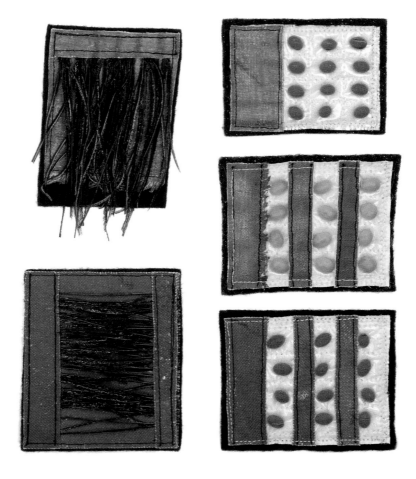

Morag Dean's tiny treasures include these brooches incorporating seeds and shells.

Morag Dean

A DELIGHT IN THE DETAILS OF NATURE IS TRANSLATED INTO 'FROCK ART'
AND MINIATURE TEXTILES BY GOLDEN BAY ARTIST MORAG DEAN.

late starter at art school, Morag created a series of fantasy dresses as part of 'Swerve', the 2001 Nelson Marlborough Institute of Technology graduating exhibition held at the Suter Gallery. Based on memories of her pre-school years in Paremata, north of Wellington, in the fifties she combined the style of dress she recalls wearing with special and potent objects from the environment she has known all her life. The result is work that charms the viewer and reviewers, with the *Nelson Mail* calling it 'simply exquisite, enigmatic and beautiful'. Yet Morag's work also has an element of danger in the sharpness of some of the contents of the fragile pockets. The works are held together with needlework, a reference to the white-on-white embroidery of Morag's forebears from Scandinavia and Britain.

Stiffened Petticoat (page 59) incorporates crab claws; *Party Frock* (page 58) uses tiny purple shells and lichen stitched into pockets of silk organza to create a layer of checks over a calico skirt. The series also includes a seed dress with akeake and kowhai creating a floral pattern and kaka-beak seeds making a border; a tutu of gorse prickles and muslin, and a 'pleated skirt' of hedgehog prickles.

Fascinated with texture and the intimate details of the small treasures she gathers on her travels, Morag has made 'quilts' of pipi shells, stones, crab claws, kowhai seeds, akeake and acacia seeds — the 'special magical objects' with which she would fill her pockets as a child — some of them displayed on beds of driftwood gathered from Nelson's Rabbit Island. She uses layers, windows, colour, stitch, light and shadows to build up a pattern with these simple materials.

All these elements are also incorporated into tiny wearable miniatures, more abstract but just as appealing in their use of natural patterns, and backed with felt so that the hedgehog prickles and shells don't scratch the wearer. Using tweezers and other small tools to make them, Morag says she needs to be 'very quiet and focused' during this process.

Morag's mother was a keen tramper and instilled a love of plants in her daughter. 'So I have always paid attention to these things,' she says. Once her mother saw Morag's artwork with the seeds she started collecting things for her. 'It was lovely — I would get little packets in the mail.'

Morag also used natural tokens for her contribution to the textile installations marking the 2004 centenary of Isel House at Stoke, Nelson — a *Cicada Curtain*, with just the cast-off skins floating within a stitched grid, and a pair of *Mahoe Curtains*, which encapsulate skeletons of mahoe leaves within a stitched grid. What better way to evoke thoughts of the many people who have been part of the life of the old house and garden?

Morag trained as an occupational therapist just as that profession was moving away from fluffy bunnies and hooked rugs — which was ironic, since the reason she went into it was because she loved craft. 'Then it became rehab and boring things like how you do your housework.' But she did learn a range of crafts such as pottery and weaving.

While living in Golden Bay she made designer windsocks, wove harakeke, worked in felt, made pottery and brought up a son with several disabilities. But her formal art training had to wait until 1998 when she began her course in Nelson, graduating in mixed media textiles in the last year of the diploma course. She passed with distinction and won the BNZ Award of Excellence, topping the arts graduates. She then worked at Nelson's Red Gallery, where she learned picture framing and acted as a gallery assistant, as well as producing work for an

Party Frock features pockets of tiny purple shells and lichen.

exhibition each year.

In 2005 she moved back to Takaka, where she is currently employed as a mental health support worker. Morag helps run an art group for her clients, and is in the process of making a 'beautiful, large studio space' suitable for teaching small groups, as well as continuing with her own work, in a huge shed on her property. She has plans to establish a cottage industry making designer floor rugs.

She continues to use the dress and quilt structures to express childhood stories, dreams, memories and emotions. 'Stitch connects me with my childhood.' ∎

Stiffened Petticoat *incorporates crab claws in its frothy layers.*

'Stitch connects me with my childhood.'

Anne Field

ANNE FIELD WAS EIGHT YEARS OLD WHEN SHE DID HER FIRST PIECE OF WEAVING — A SCARF — AND FELL IN LOVE WITH THE CRAFT. AT NINETEEN, SHE GOT HER GRANDFATHER TO MAKE HER A RIGID-HEDDLE LOOM. NOW, SHE IS ONE OF THE COUNTRY'S MOST EXPERIENCED WEAVERS AND CERTAINLY THE MOST PUBLISHED, YET SHE IS PROBABLY BETTER KNOWN OVERSEAS THAN AT HOME.

RIGHT: Grandmother's Buttons 2 *honours those women who salvaged their buttons from garments destined for the ragbag.*

 nne Field — Christchurch-based teacher, lecturer and author (five books so far, with two more on the way) — takes workshops in New Zealand and intermittently overseas: in 2006 Australia and the South Island; in 2007 the UK. However, like other members of the 45-strong Professional Weavers' Network of New Zealand, she has a low profile here.

One of a generation of Kiwi kids who benefited from educator Gordon Tovey's enlightened art and crafts syllabus, Anne's career took root on one of the two-way looms that schools had in abundance in the fifties. It wasn't a love that extended to all textile crafts, however — she hated embroidery, although she has always made her own clothes.

When Anne married Edward Field, who photographs the work for her books, the couple moved from Timaru to Christchurch and rented a flat off internationally known tapestry weaver, Ida Lough. Ida was a good role model, demonstrating that weaving could be an art form and a career, not just a hobby.

But it was spinning, rather than weaving, that Anne became interested in next. It wasn't until she was living on the West Coast in the late sixties, pregnant with her third child and 'very busy', that she decided she needed something for her brain, and weaving would be the thing.

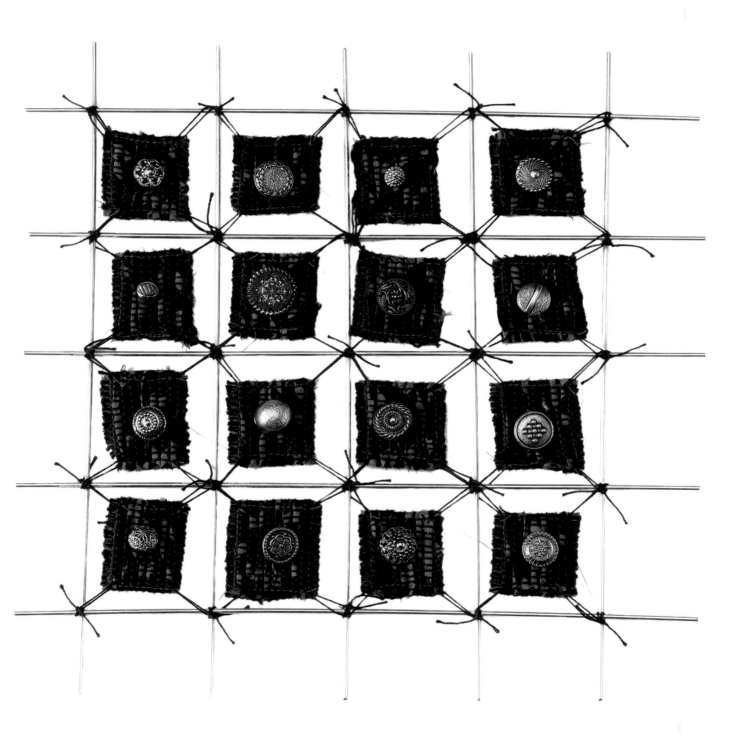

'I came back to Christchurch one weekend, bought a loom and a funny little book on weaving, and taught myself to weave.'

'I came back to Christchurch one weekend, bought a loom and a funny little book on weaving, and taught myself to weave,' she says.

In the seventies, when all handcrafts became popular, everyone was weaving 'rough sack-like things'. By then Anne wanted to make something sculptural. She entered two pieces in the Hansells Sculpture competition — a big event in those days — and had both accepted. 'When everybody got very practical I went way out,' she says. 'I always needed something new to keep me interested.'

Collapse weave is what everybody is doing now — Anne has authored a book on the subject coming out from Longacre Press in 2006, and she is also working on a book about devore (from the French word for devour). This is the process of using plant and non-plant fibre together, then removing some of the plant fibre with chemicals to leave a mix of textured and transparent areas. It's currently her most popular workshop, but she says there's still quite a bit of research to be done on different fibres before the book on devore will be finished. 'I get ideas in the middle of the night!' she laughs.

Although silk workers have been doing devore 'for ages', as far as Anne knows she is the only practitioner working in other fibres. Newer fibres, such as lyocell and polyester,

Anne Field: self-taught weaver, teacher, lecturer and author in her studio at the Arts Centre in Christchurch.

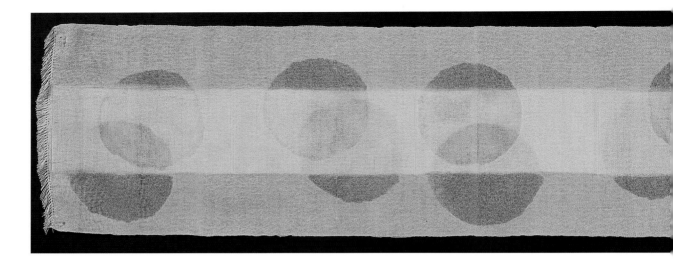

make exciting and unusual wraps, scarves and hangings. 'The nice thing about devore is that it's fairly plain weaving; you don't need a terribly complicated technique. But it pushes your design skills a lot, and you do need to know a fair bit about fibre.' Anne says it's possible to be very subtle with devore using cottons and linens.

A black wool and red cotton hanging entered in the 2006 national Creative Fibre exhibition had the look of black oriental characters on red. It's possible to create decorative and large pieces, such as big banners, but they need to be freehanging, in front of a window, for example, or well lit, so the light shines through to show the layers.

Grandmother's Buttons 2 (page 61) is Anne's tribute to the thrifty older generations who snipped off all the buttons on a garment they were going to throw into the rag bag and recycled them. 'These buttons all came from a huge collection inherited by my daughter,' she says. 'The fabric backing is rag weaving — again a recycling, something once done as a necessity with worn out clothing but now seen as fashionable.'

Anne works five days a week at her studio in Christchurch's Arts Centre — her brother Harvey Bray sells his pots there on Fridays, and Edward looks after the shop on Saturdays. Anne's computerised sixteen-shaft AVL loom allows her to do what she says weavers used to have to do with graph paper. Although it may take a whole day to enter very long patterns on the computer — and Anne still lifts the shafts with foot power and throws the shuttle — the real bonus is being able to design her own patterns and create multi-layered fabrics.

'A huge number of weavers use "recipes" from books,' she says. 'Weaving is very mathematical. But a good weaver really needs a mix of both logic and colour sense.'

Although Anne has been weaving most of her life, the joy is that there is always something new to learn. 'I can never say that I know it all,' she says. 'There are new developments in fibres, looms and techniques happening all the time. And weaving is a skill that uses all your senses — your mind, eyes and hands are all working together to make something unique.' ∎

Inner Circles *uses the devore technique on cotton-covered polyester to reveal its pattern when washed.*

A collapse weave scarf using fine merino over twisted wool.

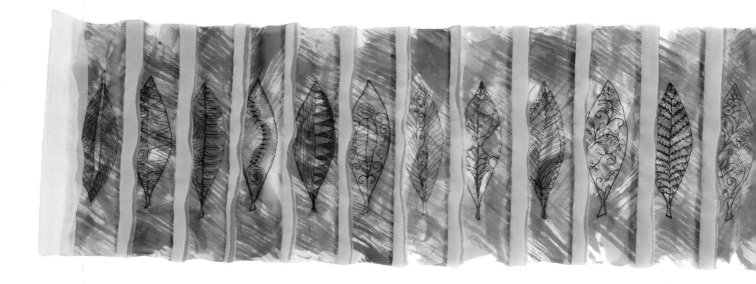

Maree Garstang

How to convey the emotional impact of the New Zealand bush — that was the challenge Maree Garstang grappled with for many years, before she began using layers of nylon sheer to construct her 'meditative' hangings.

 aree's love of the bush had its roots in childhood, when she lived in Birkenhead, on Auckland's North Shore. The family property had three-quarters of an acre of bush, 'where we played games and climbed trees. Even back then I would seek out times to sit in the branches of a tree and dream'.

Later, after marrying and moving to Masterton, Maree and her husband Tony, a lawyer, spent a lot of time tramping in the Tararua Ranges, and still do occasionally. It helps that their home at Upper Plain, west of the town, looks out toward the ranges. 'The Tararuas

Process of Travel I —
an interpretation of Maree Garstang's
'ethereal feelings' about the New
Zealand bush.

are always there, and they're so beautiful,'
Maree says.

However, Maree is not the ideal tramping
companion. While her husband likes to keep
going until he reaches the mountaintops, Maree
would rather sit in one spot and 'feel' the bush.
Until recently, conveying that overwhelming
emotion in fabric was just too hard.

'For many years I couldn't deal with it,'
Maree says. 'I was always aware of how other
embroiderers were interpreting it, but my
feelings about it were quite ethereal — the
complexity, layers, the different strata of moss,
trunks . . . all the way to the treetops. It relates

to the human being too, and your awareness of
yourself.'

It was Trevor Morris at Wairarapa
Polytechnic who helped Maree break away from
her stuck situation. 'Ask yourself, what if you
combined this with that?' he suggested. 'Find out
what happens. If it fails it fails.' It's a question
Maree now asks herself often, something to fall
back on when she needs to find a way to progress.

For Maree, planting bush on their own
piece of land has been an attempt to recreate her
childhood environment but, she says, 'You can't
recreate 100 years of it, the smell of the ground
that you breathe in'.

As a kindergarten teacher Maree always wanted to paint with her charges. After marrying and moving south at the age of 23, it was to be another ten years before she saw an exhibition of embroidery works and decided, 'This is for me!' From that exhibition grew the Wairarapa Embroiderers' Guild, of which she was a founding member.

'I learned most of my techniques through the guild — I covered most, dabbling in some and enthusiastically immersing myself in others,' she says. 'I was very thankful to be offered a range of workshops — the guild was absolutely brilliant in that way.' She used surface stitchery a lot in her early works; canvas work was another love, and the cross-stitch kits she designed and sold paid her fees at Wairarapa Polytechnic.

While she will use any of those techniques to get the right image in her work, Maree is mostly self-taught in the techniques she now uses predominantly — machine stitching and heat-set printing, where she paints on paper and heat-sets that onto nylon voile. 'It's the only satisfactory way of printing on nylon,' she says (see *Process of Travel I* and *II*, page 67 and 68).

Maree does a lot of drawing, carrying a notebook and pasting scraps of paper into her workbook when she returns to her craft-filled home. Chairs painted by Maree, stunning furniture by her son-in-law Mike Hindmarsh, from Nelson, and textiles everywhere make for an inspirational environment. Maree has always been very aware of fabric. Her mother and grandmother were both embroiderers, and she

Process of Travel II
— *the second in a series using nylon voile to convey the fleeting aspects of a bush walk.*

realises she must have been encouraged to play with fabric as a child, to discover for herself 'how fabric moves and how you can manipulate it'.

As well as exhibiting with the New Zealand Embroiderers' Guild and the Combined Textiles of New Zealand group, Maree continues to have solo shows at Aratoi, Masterton's art gallery and museum, and at Greytown's Heart of Glass. 'In the past it's been hard for textile artists to be taken seriously,' she says. 'Today there is greater recognition and appreciation of art in textiles.' ◼

'I learned most of my techniques through the guild — I covered most, dabbling in some and enthusiastically immersing myself in others.'

Merrilyn George

MERRILYN GEORGE HAS LIVED UNDER THE SHADOW OF
MT RUAPEHU VIRTUALLY ALL HER LIFE. IT IS NO WONDER,
THEN, THAT THE MOUNTAIN AND THE LAND AROUND IT
DOMINATE HER THINKING AND HER QUILTS.

 errilyn was born in Horopito (where the film *Smash Palace* was made) and moved with her family to Ohakune, where she now lives, when she was seven years old. A few years living with her parents in the forest camp at Minginui, three years studying in Otago and five years teaching art at Feilding's Hato Paora College is the extent of her time away from her home territory.

Merrilyn has been a teacher now for 40 years, and has always loved secondary teaching. Trained in Home Economics, she first taught homecraft and clothing but has since taught 'almost everything except English — and I keep threatening the department I'll do that!' A competent speaker of te reo, she has taught Maori language for many years. Although not Maori herself, she says almost everybody she's related to is, including her husband Ken.

A former assistant principal, Merrilyn is currently Head of Technology, Textiles and Food, and the Specialist Classroom Teacher

Tangiwai is a tribute to those who died in the 1953 rail disaster near Ohakune.

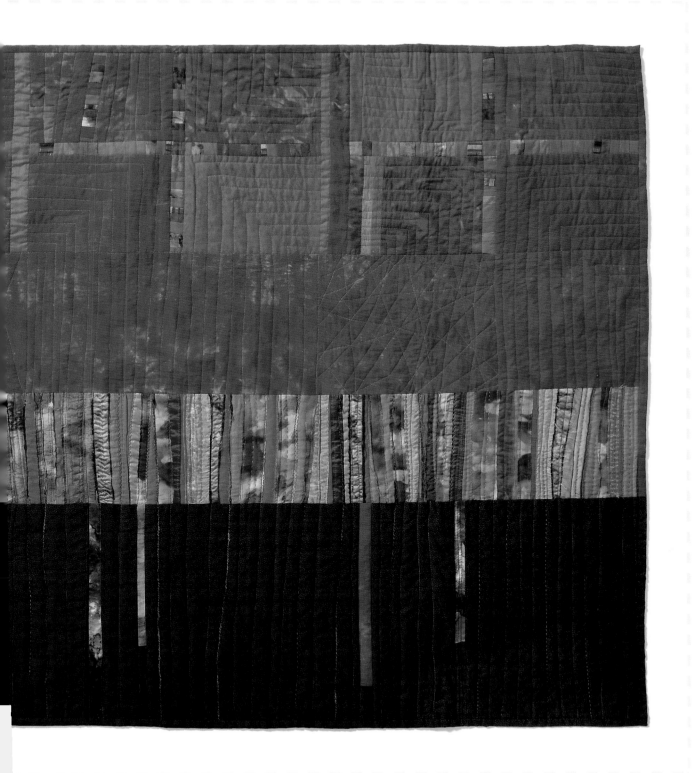

RIGHT: **The Tin Shed** *captures the essence of rusted farm huts in the countryside around Ohakune, where quilter Merrilyn George (left) lives and works.*

at Ruapehu College. She now teaches the grandchildren of pupils she taught in her first years at the college. 'It is a real joy to be following families, and they appreciate it too.'

When she finished secondary school, Merrilyn wanted to study art but was advised not to by her principal. 'I think it was not considered a field for young ladies then,' she says. Also, no one in her immediate family had ever entered tertiary study. In retrospect, she thinks it was wise advice.

She has always sewn, even as a girl, but her daughter was a quilter before Merrilyn started. It wasn't until a 1997 symposium in Hamilton that her quilt art started to take off. She won Best

Wall Quilt for *Nga Whare Maunga II* (Mountain Houses), which showed views of Ruapehu erupting, through the skeleton structure of a traditional Maori house.

A Science, Mathematics and Technology Fellowship, awarded by the Royal Society of New Zealand, allowed Merrilyn to take a year off in 2002 to research technological changes in traditional and modern fibre — including paper-making, hemp-growing and the use of mud in piupiu and cloak dyeing. She worked with weavers and the commercial flax industry, and at Whanganui Museum researched the fibres and technologies introduced by European colonists, such as wool, twine and candlewick.

'I would sit with a korowai and think about the hands that painstakingly crafted the work, I felt in union with the makers. It was a very spiritual experience.'

Then she took the technology that was used for dyeing the muka (flax fibres) black, and transferred that knowledge to trial mud painting on cotton.

Using the idea of a korowai or cloak to express her ideas, Merrilyn's hemp quilt *Kaitaka I* (pictured right) is one of a series made in response to the year's immersion in the museum taonga (treasures). 'I would sit with a korowai and think about the hands that painstakingly crafted the work,' she says. 'I felt in union with the makers. It was a very spiritual experience.' Later works in the series use mud to make patterns on the reverse of the quilts, including some from a paru (mud) pit on family land.

Merrilyn keeps her substantial stash of fabric at school and shares it with her students. 'I've had it so long, I've moved away from popular fabrics,' she says. 'I'm often redyeing, dipping or printing over cloth or writing on it with textile ink.' Stamps, computer prints and printer's type are all used to add words to quilts, such as the list of those who died in the Tangiwai disaster, on the reverse of *Tangiwai* (page 71). 'I put my heart and soul into that,' she says, 'both sides'.

Even with a long teaching day, Merrilyn manages to structure her routine so she gets uninterrupted time on her quilts. 'I'm a finisher,' she says. 'And I'm quite good at deadlines. I'm driven.' When working on a project she can prepare meals and lessons for a week, homework for her pupils, get up at 4 a.m.

to put in three hours before school, then do three more at the end of the day. She loves the composition stage of putting together a quilt, and the hand and machine quilting, but not 'the boring stuff in between'.

With school resources available as well as her own, she uses a range of sewing machines, from a 1903 treadle, the trusty, old school Bernina 801, to her own Bernina 1630. 'I love treadling. It reminds me of my early years teaching, when we used to sew first thing to warm ourselves up!'

Merrilyn has now set up a small gallery, Whare a Toi, in Miro St, Ohakune. She is currently working on a little series of 'living treasures'. The first is 99-year-old Annie Creighton, who lives in a 'very colonial' house in Merrilyn's street. 'She knew my grandmother, who died in 1918 in the flu pandemic.' Two younger women from the local marae will also be featured, one with her guitar and the other the karakia (prayer) bell, which is rung at seven, morning and night.

Now involved in Treaty settlement discussions regarding the passing of Ohakune and district to the Crown in the 1880s, Merrilyn finds she is looking at covenants and treaties, agreements and disagreements as themes for her quilts. 'I love the history of this place,' she says. 'My dad was a great storyteller and he used to take me on his knee and call me his mate. It's all tied together with the mountain and the land. They all interact.' ∎

Kaitaka I *is the first in a series inspired by taonga in the Whanganui Museum.*

Chelsea Gough

A PRINTMAKER BY TRAINING, CHELSEA GOUGH BEGAN USING TEXTILES WHEN SHE WAS ARTIST-IN-RESIDENCE AT WHANGANUI POLYTECHNIC. TIRED OF THE TWO-DIMENSIONAL NATURE OF PRINTS ON PAPER, SHE SOURCED BLANKETS LOCALLY AND PRINTED ON THEM USING WOODCUTS AND ETCHINGS, ADDING STITCHES FOR EMPHASIS.

RIGHT: A bird cannot fly without its feathers.

 New Zealander who was raised in Melbourne, Chelsea completed a two-year diploma in visual arts at the Box Hill Institute of TAFE, before a three-year degree in printmaking at the Victorian College of Arts, University of Melbourne. Then, feeling she didn't want to study for a while, she decided to find out more about the country her parents had grown up in and travelled to Wellington.

Having already started researching ideas of identity during her degree course, Chelsea spent her mornings at the Alexander Turnbull Library's photographic archive and afternoons discovering the city with her friend Gabby O'Connor, who had also just arrived from Melbourne.

Showing her work to the New Zealand design store Kura led to an invitation to a printmaking wananga at Whanganui Polytechnic and eventually to Chelsea moving to New Zealand for her residency there for the 2002 academic year. As artist-in-residence, she taught students as well as working on her own art, and also experimented with photo-etching on copper,

Somewhere Over the Rainbow features a woodcut print of Taranaki on an old wool blanket.

during a workshop with Scottish printmaker Stuart Duffin. In a press-building workshop, she learned how to use various engineering machines to make her own etching and relief-printing press.

Over the following two years Chelsea was programme co-ordinator and lectured in visual arts at Wellington Institute of Technology (Weltec) in Petone, and tutored at Pablos Art Studio in Wellington.

Chelsea says she has never been particularly interested in painting, preferring the practicality — 'the hands-on activity' — that goes with printmaking. Printing on blankets takes tactility one step further. 'I began to be really interested in things about home and home-making and domesticity, which brought me to crafty things. It started at a time of my life when I was most transient but there was an underlying sense that I was home.'

'I began to be really interested in things about home and home-making and domesticity, which brought me to crafty things. It started at a time of my life when I was most transient but there was an underlying sense that I was home.'

She is interested in how children gain an understanding about issues such as land rights, and how ideas about confiscation can be communicated. As well as embroidering the coastline and rivers of Taranaki in the blanket works (opposite), Chelsea has stitched in the boundaries of confiscated land. The prints were made by transferring photographic postcards onto wood, then making woodcuts to print onto the blanket. The whakatauaki, or proverb, applied to the work, 'Ma te huruhuru te manu e rere', which translates as 'A bird cannot fly without its feathers', was given to Chelsea by a Maori colleague at Whanganui Polytechnic, Marilyn Vreede.

Somewhere Over the Rainbow features a woodcut of Taranaki, the mountain. 'It is about communicating a sense of optimisim,' she says. 'I was thinking about how education is so important in the development of a culture, especially in relation to the way in which a bicultural society understands itself.'

While Chelsea doesn't speak te reo Maori, she has been invited to hui such as the 2004 Printmakers' Hui at Te Wananga o Aotearoa in Auckland. This helped her establish networks with Maori printmakers within New Zealand, and meet First Peoples printmakers from North America.

As a consequence of meeting people in Wanganui before she moved to New Zealand, she was invited by Toi Maori Aotearoa to participate in 'He Rere Kee — Taking Flight', a 2004 New Zealand Festival exhibition at Tinakori Gallery.

'A lot of people seem to have seen that,' she says. 'It was a turning point in public awareness for me. You don't know what to expect when you're invited to take part in group exhibitions. You work in isolation, you send the work in and you turn up at the opening — and all these people you enjoy talking to are there. It's very nice to be invited to be part of these shows. They have had an influence on the way my life has worked out.'

The year 2005 brought inclusion in two group shows at City Gallery Wellington's Michael Hirschfeld Gallery, 'Manawa Taki — The Pulsing Heart', curated by Sarah Farrar, and 'Postmark', an artist project by Gabby O'Connor.

Chelsea most recently collaborated with Gabby on a work for the recent New Zealand exhibition 'Jewellery Out of Context' at Sydney's Muse Gallery, in which thread and pins were used to make a delicate web of pattern on a sofa. She plans to create something similar on a wall at Cuckoo (formerly Pipi), the Greytown café she and her partner Tim Wellington now own and operate. A spotty room with doilies is another possibility. Whichever way Chelsea Gough goes, there's bound to be a domestic element in her work for some time to come. ∎

A crocheted tea party fit for royalty — complete with kiwifruit-topped pav and saveloys with tomato sauce . . .

Jacquelyn Greenbank

WHEN SHE COULDN'T AFFORD TO BUY A MODEL ROYAL CARRIAGE AND HORSES FROM AN ANTIQUE SHOP, AVID ROYAL WATCHER JACQUELYN GREENBANK DECIDED TO MAKE HER OWN — IN CROCHET.

growing up in a crafty family — her dad taught her to knit and her mum taught her to do French knitting — Jacquelyn Greenbank nevertheless didn't learn to crochet until she was into her honours year at the University of Canterbury's School of Fine Arts. She discovered she could build a little form out of crochet 'by looping them back onto each other and building on it'.

That was the beginning of her three-dimensional fibre pieces. Now she 'paints' with a crochet hook and yarn, and 'draws' with thread and needle — convincingly enough to pass her Masters degree (MFA) with distinction in painting, and to win the People's Choice at the National Drawing Award, exhibited at Auckland's Artspace and The Physics Room in Christchurch, for her embroidered drawing of the Queen Mother. The 'drawing' was featured in *Staple* magazine.

Before long, the obsessive crocheter had to adapt her techniques to include the use of recycled ready-made textiles. 'It's really time-consuming to make, and quite expensive to buy wool. Lots of people think I have made a pattern — they think I'm damned clever — but I'm just cutting and pasting.' However, there is a considerable amount of technical skill involved in covering a bicycle and crash helmet, creating a woollen replica of a crown or constructing a model of the Pink and White Terraces (not to mention organising the electrics so it fizzes and lights up). Jacquelyn does admit to being an obsessive-compulsive person who likes to do things with her hands all the time. 'Painting's a really isolating craft, but with crochet you can build up little pieces when you're with other people.'

Jacquelyn has always been into royalty — 'Lady Diana's wedding and princess and fairytale ideals, that whole scenario'. She fell in love with a model of the coronation coach and horses — 'quite a big one' — in the window of a Christchurch antique shop, but it was too expensive for her. She made one in crochet, with a tiny landscape (the island of Greenbank)

'Painting's a really isolating craft, but with crochet you can build up little pieces when you're with other people.'

and exhibited it while still at art school. When it was poorly displayed, a tutor challenged her to take control of the whole process, so she started providing everything covered in crochet, sending her work ready to display exactly as it should be seen. Now things like plinths, electric extension cords and plugs are completely encased in crochet.

By the time Jacquelyn graduated, her Masters exhibition showed a whole Royal Tour, from the carriage down to the tea party, complete with the food HRH might have been offered on her tour of provincial New Zealand — pavlova with kiwifruit, sandwiches and chocolate biscuits — not forgetting the carnations in vases complete with royal crest.

Her irrepressible sense of humour — she laughs a lot of the time — is obviously what makes Jacquelyn's work so popular. 'They know it's going to be crochet covered so they check me out to see if I've done everything right.' She doesn't feel disadvantaged by the humour in her work — and certainly doesn't like to take herself too seriously. 'It's firstly craft art and then humour,' she says.

Jacquelyn is still following her royal theme

— next up is a barbecue, with pork chops, eggs, sausages and mushrooms. Everything is in fifties royal colours — red, white, blue and gold; not jewel-encrusted but definitely gold-encrusted — with HM's logo or initials.

Two exhibitions in Melbourne in association with the Commonwealth Games were great fun. One was at the University of Melbourne's VCA Gallery; the other was at the docks, in one of 44 containers stacked up on top of each other with access via walkways. Jacquelyn's partner Jamie Richardson, a visual artist, shared her container, along with two other Christchurch artists.

It suits Jacquelyn that her work continues to be widely exhibited. 'I try and show it as much as possible — it takes such a long time to make!' However, now that her work is known she can be a little more selective. 'There's a lot of groundwork involved in sending out work to build up an audience,' she says. 'Now I hope I've got one and can make them wait a bit. Then I can make more [for each show]'. ■

. . . and sandwiches to start with.

Bronwyn Griffiths

A HOOKED RAG RUG BOUGHT IN HAMILTON SOME 40 YEARS AGO GAVE BRONWYN GRIFFITHS THE IDEA THAT SHE TOO COULD MAKE SOMETHING LOVELY, AND FUNCTIONAL, OUT OF SCRAPS. HOWEVER, IT WAS ANOTHER 20 YEARS BEFORE SHE BEGAN WEAVING HER OWN RUGS.

 spinner and handweaver from the age of 20, Bronwyn has collected textiles all of her life. She learned to spin in Auckland and moved on to weaving from there. But it wasn't until two decades ago that she moved from weaving with bought yarns and her own handspun wool, to using recycled fabric.

Bronwyn, who trained as an occupational therapist, laments the loss of the looms that most hospitals used to have. She 'quivers and quavers' between an upright rug loom and a floor loom in the verandah studio of her Eastbourne home, using both to weave tufted floor rugs in wool, and flat mats in cottons, rayons and silks. Cut-up denims from her current project litter the floor beneath one loom; other clothes are roughly colour-coded in large, open shelves. Coats, jackets and dressing gowns are all thrown in the washing machine before use, to check for colourfastness, and line-dried in the old-fashioned way on wire lines propped up to

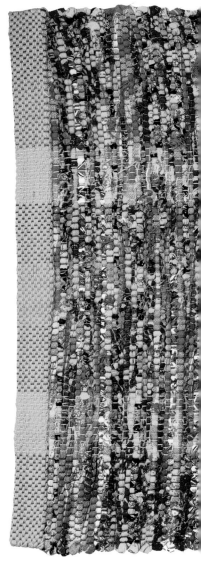

A tablemat finely woven using strips of cotton.

catch the breeze.

It's like stepping back in time here. Just a street away from Wellington Harbour, every inch of ground in her sunny backyard is covered in herbs, vegetables, fruit trees and flowers, a joyful profusion that brings back memories of Grandmother's country garden. In keeping

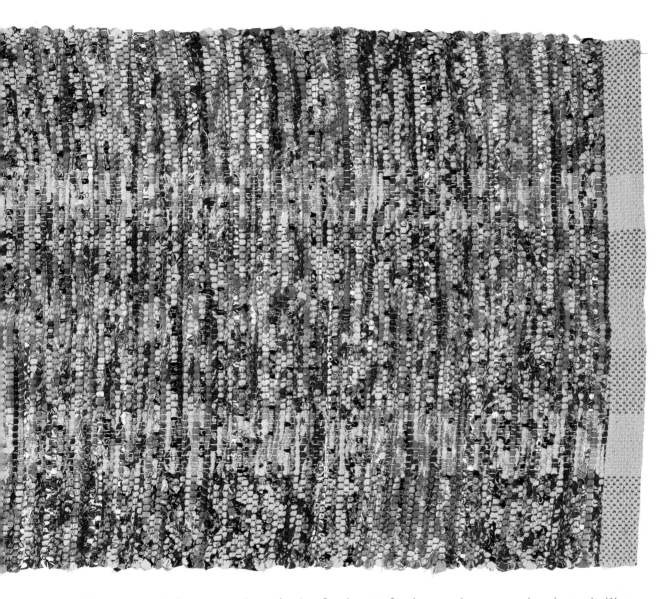

Bronwyn sticks to wool or denim for her tufted rugs, because she doesn't like the mix of textures. Tweeds are among her favourites, for the added interest produced by the fleck. Old skirts, suits and dresses found at school and church fairs are sized up for colour and fibre content.

with the recycling ethic, Brownwyn's lifestyle is one of self-sufficiency. There's no phone or television and she eats what she grows and preserves, assisted by the flock of chooks she has kept for years — Rhode Island Reds, Plymouth Rocks, handsome and primitive Aracanas (which lay blue eggs), White Sussex and fluffy black bantams. In turn, her hens provide her with organic eggs for the English muffins she makes on her woodstove, and manure for the compost.

As well as textile treasures — embroidered laundry bags on coathangers, sacking aprons, dressmakers' accessories and crochet cushions — there are special pieces of furniture found in skips and refurbished, a collection of old willow washing baskets, and in the kitchen, tin and enamelware and small wall cabinets.

The house's wooden floors are covered in vintage hooked rugs Bronwyn has collected over the years, the most recent on a trip to Yorkshire, where she found three. 'I can't see the point of not using them,' she says. 'Even the ugly ones are nice! They're mostly wool, though they used to mix cotton and rayon in as well.' All can be washed, the wool ones by hand in the bath as they are too big and heavy to go in the washing machine.

Bronwyn sticks to wool or denim for her tufted rugs, because she doesn't like the mix of textures. Tweeds are among her favourites, for the added interest produced by the fleck. Old skirts, suits and dresses found at school and church fairs are sized up for colour and fibre content — she mostly chooses wool or cotton, though sometimes silk slips in if it's a desirable colour. The tufts are made from woollen strips

knotted over two linen warp threads, often in a simple geometric pattern — made without a pattern for the first half, then carefully counted as she continues on the mirror image to the end.

The flat weave produces beautifully marled and superbly washable tablemats, bath mats, cushions and floor coverings, restricted in size not just by the width of the loom but because of the need to wash them comfortably. 'You can make two or three and stitch them together, as they do in Scandinavia,' she says, 'but they're a bit big to wash, and the stitching gets a bit fragile'.

Too stunning to be called 'rag rugs' — a woven, tufted rug of recycled woollens and a flat-weave cotton table runner.

She also makes braided rugs, where three strands of recycled cloth are plaited together, then laid flat and stitched into a round or oval shape especially suited to chair cushions.

Bronwyn's two spinning wheels are used in fits and starts, but only to produce yarn to knit up for her own use. 'It's a bit lumpy but I like the texture and it's soothing to do,' she says. She uses her sewing machine to make up the cushions, and has invested in tougher denim needles to cope with the heavy fabric often requested in commissions. About half of Bronwyn's work is commisioned, the rest sells at exhibitions.

While she often dyes clothes for her own use, sometimes using dyes from her garden, Bronwyn doesn't do that with her rug rags. 'I'm very careful about colours — I don't think there's anything worse than one colour bleeding into another.'

On her daily walks along the harbour's edge with friends who also love textiles and history, or while cycling to the village shops, Bronwyn keeps an eye out for opportunities for recycling — and not just from skips outside houses undergoing renovation. It's a lifestyle that perfectly suits someone in tune with the seasons. ■

*The beader's art lends itself
to articles of adornment.*

Katya Gunn

KATYA GUNN THINKS SHE WOULD HAVE BEEN LITTLE MORE THAN
FOUR YEARS OLD WHEN SHE FIRST STARTED NEEDLEWORK. SKILLED
IN A WIDE RANGE OF TEXTILES, KATYA WAS BLESSED WITH A
MOTHER, GRANDMOTHER AND GREAT-GRANDMOTHER WHO WERE ALL
NEEDLEWORKERS.

he Dunedin-based embroiderer's
European heritage was coloured
early on with indigenous influences.
Holidays spent in Fiji with her
maternal grandmother involved 'a strange mix
of tropical island craft — the native weavers out
the back — and the last of the colonial ladies with
their embroidery'. Holidays at Turangi, where
her ecologist father stayed at Papakai Marae while
researching the impact of the Tongariro power
scheme on native fish, allowed Katya to spend
time with the flax weavers.

'I have always wanted to make things that
were usable,' she says. 'There is a richness and
depth of meaning in utilitarian function, and I
think the most vibrant arts are those with a strong
element of utility.'

A collector of 'little things with holes in'
since she was tiny, Katya has, for the last fifteen
years or so chosen to work increasingly with
beads, on pieces that take weeks to create. 'Bead
embroidery allows you to use beads of almost any
size to completely cover, or just delicately adorn,
fabric,' she says. She luxuriates in the slow
process of transferring the pattern stitch by stitch
onto a background fabric, absorbing the feel of
the fabric and how the thread is working. 'There
is time to think about what you are doing. It's a
completely different time scale.'

At home in her dim workroom, Katya
operates in a six-inch pool of light which creates
a restfulness befitting the tiny scale on which she
works. 'Even if I'm working on something bigger
I'm only doing a tiny bit at a time.'

She usually starts with a quote or some
piece of language, and either draws a design
or conjures up an image from something she's
seen. *The Shoe Book* was based on sample books
and Belle Epoque catalogues for court dresses.
Each 'page' has a letter of the alphabet. On the
back of a bag beaded with Edvard Munch's *The
Scream* is a quote: 'When you look long into the
abyss, the abyss looks into you'.

'Nothing comes from nothing,' Katya says;

'even if you think it's completely original, it always harks back to something you've seen'.

It was an older embroiderer, octogenarian Jean Hart, who encouraged Katya on the beading trail, fifteen years ago. 'She had quite a lot of old beads and she had seen a lot of inspiring new work from the States. Beading is so universal — there are examples all around the world.'

Then a piece of wisdom from Kaffe Fassett encouraged her to design her own patterns — you can copy and enjoy that, but you can also create your own. Katya says she was also inspired by tales of her grandmother, who personalised her daughters' dresses. 'I was excited by the idea that this was an OK thing to do,' she says. 'The more I started doing it, the more enjoyment I got out of doing my own thing.'

Her tiny, beaded bowls representing *The Seven Deadly Sins* are created using colours traditionally associated with the sins in medieval church paintings. Sloth, Greed, Anger, Pride, Envy, Lust and Gluttony each hold one of Prudentius' (c. 410) 'Contrary Virtues', pearls of wisdom which protect against the deadly sins — Diligence, Liberality, Patience, Humility, Kindness, Chastity and Abstinence.

As well as creating works from beads alone — connecting the tiny pieces of glass with thread — Katya increasingly enjoys tambour beading, a couture technique used in France, where the beads are strung onto a thread and hooked onto the fabric one by one. 'I love the sense of history in tambour beading — it has origins in both India and China — and I love the way it gives a more fluid line than simply sewing onto a background. The irony of it is that this was the original production line; now cornelli machines do that, although they can't manage lots of colour changes.'

Katya works two days a week as a sexual health doctor. Although she spent time in her general training stitching up emergency cases under a pool of light, she says the main connection between her work now with mostly healthy young people and her art is that both reflect her interest in human nature.

In 2005, Katya and her family moved into a splendidly baronial house and garden close to the heart of town, which lends itself to occasions such as the medieval banquet held for family and friends. For one steeped in history, she is surprisingly web-literate — in one of the house's large rooms there is a bank of computers on which her husband and son design websites.

Katya's site www.Lucellan.com takes its name from the word that gives us luxurious. Lucellus was a Roman general who lived to enjoy a life of great extravagance after retiring from public life around 63 BC. While hardly reflective of her lifestyle, luxury is something Katya Gunn can create through her art. ■

Katya Gunn in her Dunedin studio — practice makes perfect.

'I love the sense of history in tambour beading — it has origins in both India and China — and I love the way it gives a more fluid line than simply sewing onto a background.'

Megan Hansen-Knarhoi

AFTER HER ACADEMIC CAREER CULMINATED IN A DOUBLE DEGREE IN ANTHROPOLOGY AND ART HISTORY, WITH A FURTHER BA (HONOURS) IN ART HISTORY, MEGAN HANSEN-KNARHOI DECIDED THAT MAKING ART WAS PREFERABLE TO WRITING ABOUT IT.

Wool, woollen objects and the techniques used for making them have fascinated Megan since childhood. Playing in the back bedroom with her granny's recycled wool, she was happiest rewinding the balls of unravelled yarn from outgrown jerseys in mint green, orange and yellow, from which her grandma then made little dresses for her dolls.

You can see where Megan's work — complete with loose ends — is coming from. Where it's going to is not so comfortable. Her stated aim is to examine and juxtapose themes of domestic and ecclesiastical ritual. Her latest work *Crotchtit* — an edgy pun — gives new meaning to the term 'soft porn'. The viewer is seduced by the variegated cotton wrapping, and memories of those boxes made of old Christmas cards held together by crochet, before seeing what is depicted on the outside. A softly subversive message in her trademark cruciform package, the exhibition, shown at Anna Bibby Gallery in 2005, definitely had the 'ouch' factor.

Megan's coathanger works, exhibited at Mary Newton Gallery in Wellington and in a Ponsonby Rd window 'dep_art_ment' in Auckland, are less political and more chaotic. Anyone who has ever looked closely at the hangers in op-shops will be drawn into the haphazard mayhem of the crocheted shapes — some her own work, some found. Megan says a copycat installation in another Ponsonby Rd window was the ultimate flattery.

The artist catches her viewers with kitsch — like the cute, yellow baby chick egg warmers she made for the Rose Griffen-curated 'Handycrafts' show, which began its national tour at te tuhi (the mark) in Pakuranga in 2003 — and

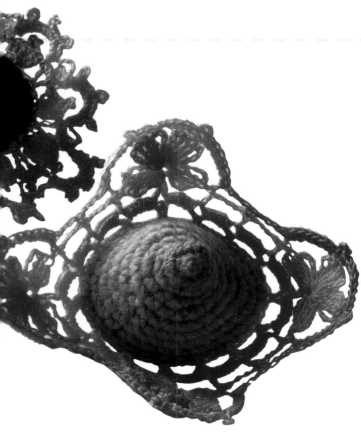

White Boob/Black Boob continues to explore the ethnic stereotypes of the Topsy/Turvy doll.

While she is trying to expand and break out of the small format, Megan is always drawn back to wool and to low art forms, and she also likes finding ways to abstract crochet forms using a variety of techniques and applications.

Currently completing her Masters in Fine Arts from Elam, Megan is enjoying playing with the ethnic theme she first explored in *Topsy/Turvy* in 2004. This is a two-way doll that has a brown and a white body joined at the midriff, clothed in the kind of dress each would have worn at the time of colonisation, complete with a cross for the Pakeha and a piece of pounamu for the Maori.

Megan has a collection of op-shop, topsy-turvy dolls, the originators of which are thought to have been African slaves who concealed their own likenesses beneath innocuous white versions. Her doll, which went to Brazil for the Sao Paulo Bienal, is not asexual either, as most are. This theme has been extended with work such as *White Boob/Black Boob* (pictured) which was included in a group show at Mary Newton Gallery in June 2006.

Every couple of years, Megan gets together with friend and fellow artist Ani Oneill — who first convinced her to become an artist rather than an academic or curator — on one of her interactive *The Buddy System* installations, an 'incredibly intensive project' that takes a lot of time, patience and love. At the Melbourne *Buddy System* in 2006, they found themselves inundated with eager crochet wannabes — the wall covered with crochet flowers engenders some wonderful moments in the making. ■

entices them to think about the implications. Of *Kit(s)ch(ick)ens* she has said, 'I made those chickens en masse because I wanted the work to look really hideous. It was reminiscent of battery farming and the mass production of life, which is then destroyed. I wanted it to be grotesque but at the same time celebrating the effort women put into these impractical objects'.

Almost all of Megan's crocheted pieces have some 'bunny wool', that fluffy stuff little girls' boleros were made from in the fifties. These include *Peppermint Piety*, in minty 'old, grandma colours' (shown at Mary Newton Gallery) to *Cry for everything bad that's ever happened*, thirteen crocheted woollen crosses spilling out of a cardboard carton. All fluffy and tufted with loose ends, *Cry* was part of Ponsonby gallery Objectspace's 'Left at the Member's Lounge' group show in 2004.

Hearts Entwined *uses randomly chosen fabric and ornate machine trapunto quilting.*

Heather Harding

'THERE'S SO MUCH AMAZING WORK BEING DONE BY NEW ZEALAND QUILTERS,' SAYS HEATHER HARDING. 'I ADMIRE THE SKILLS AND THE IMAGINATION AND HOW THEY'VE USED THE FABRIC. BUT MOST OF ALL I LOVE UTTER SIMPLICITY.'

It's the simplicity of her own quilts that has won awards for Upper Hutt quilter Heather Harding, although she doesn't shy away from using some very tricky fabrics. Now retired from school teaching, she is committed to using what she already has — a philosophy she shares with those early Durham and American Amish women who believed in 'use it up, wear it out, make it do or do without'. A primary school teacher for 34 years, Heather now has the luxury of quilting all day should she so desire. 'It's playtime all the time!' she says.

Heather is unusual in her ability to tackle the most slippery of materials, things most cotton-purist quilters would never touch — sateen, Dupion silk, duchesse satin, shantung. She loves fabrics that are more commonly associated with balldresses, bridal gowns or boudoir furnishings — even upholstery — and will often use both sides of a single material if it gives her enough colour variation on one of her classic strippy quilts.

Heather usually starts her quilts with a good look at what's in her cupboard and how she can use it. Her stash has been accumulating over many years from many sources.

Hearts Entwined (pictured) is an example where she has asked the question: 'What can I do with this?' She actually had two attempts at this quilt, first using gold polyester silk as the background in the blocks, but when it was all put together she says it looked awful. Heather is so thrifty she put it away and had another go a year later. She describes working on a quilt of 'silks and satins and silky furnishings' that is not going at all well saying 'I won't judge it till it's done, though I'm already asking "Is it worth it?"' The quilting is machined trapunto, which is stuffed from the back.

'I think you start to relax about the whole business of what fabric you use,' she says. 'When you're a beginner, you think everything has to match, but the more you worry and fuss about it, the worse it gets.'

From a tradition that predates the days of American settlement, Heather's strippy and whole-cloth quilts — where one piece of fabric is covered in elaborate running-stitch lines of

'It was the first time I had come across quilts not copied from books, and seen machine quilting done well. It was very exciting, a real eye-opener, to see work by people like Gwen Wanigasekera — I thought, my God, how did she do that piecing?'

quilting — go back to designs from Wales and County Durham, in the UK. She draws up her designs full size, on greaseproof paper stuck together with glue stick, and uses a lightbox to mark the cloth before quilting with a washable blue pencil. She prefers New Zealand wool batting for hand quilting — it's nice to quilt and doesn't crease when the quilt is folded — but uses an American Hobbs 80/20 cotton and polyester mix for machine quilting.

Heather says she is drawn to hard-to-source Durham and Welsh patterns, like the Tudor Rose, which are now found mostly in museums. She finds them ideal for interpreting quilting patterns from different cultural sources — a Pataka Porirua award-winner, which used simple broad stripes, as the Amish do, combined Maori kowhaiwhai with Celtic knot patterns. She is keen to get back to kowhaiwhai-type patterns.

What also sets Heather apart from almost every other quilter, anywhere, is that she executes hand and machine quilting equally well, and has won prizes in both techniques. In 2002, won Pataka Porirua's award for Excellence in Quilting, and the following year, at a biennial quilting symposium in Christchurch, she won eight awards with five quilts, including the peer-awarded National Association of Quilters' Award of Excellence. At the 2005 symposium in

Auckland, she won a prize for an entry featuring hand-quilted trapunto feathers (on delustred satin) and machine-quilted feathered hearts.

Heather taught herself to quilt from books in order to co-ordinate the making of a group quilt for her mother's eightieth birthday in 1977. Since then, she has done her fair share of voluntary stitching — quilts for raffles, the neonatal unit at Wellington Hospital, and replacement bedcoverings for Hutt Valley's Te Omanga Hospice.

A hobby china-painter from a large family in rural Taranaki who learned to sew on a clacking old Singer treadle machine, Heather showed her ignorance early on when she bought several metres of each colour she wanted to use in that first quilt. 'I didn't want to run out!' she laughs. 'It just shows how much I knew.' She's still using up the remnants. Copying from books, she draughted twelve-inch blocks, put fabric in packets and sent it out to her five sisters, their children and even great-grandchildren. When the blocks came back she did all the joining up and quilting. The quilt was never used — because it was 'too good' — and it came back to its maker when her mother died in 1987.

Five years ago, Heather chopped the tips off three fingers in an accident with a motor mower, not long before she won the first big Pataka

Carmen *is an example of Heather Harding's supreme skill as a hand quilter, even using non-traditional fabrics.*

award. At Hutt Hospital's plastic surgery unit she pleaded with the surgeon who, having saved two fingers, was preparing to take the first joint off the last finger. 'But you can't, I'm a quilter!' she said. 'You will adapt,' he told her. And she did. 'It was a blessing in disguise.' She now has a prosthetic thimble that fits neatly over the tip of her middle finger and the only thing she has trouble with is picking up pins.

Heather differs from many textile artists, who feel out of place in traditional guilds and groups, and her membership of Capital Quilters in Lower Hutt and Pinestream in Upper Hutt is important to her. A real turning point came

when her work was accepted for the first-ever national award for quilters, the 'Enzed' exhibition at Auckland's Aotea Centre in 1990.

'It was the first time I had come across quilts not copied from books, and seen machine quilting done well,' she says. 'It was very exciting, a real eye-opener, to see work by people like Gwen Wanigasekera — I thought, my God, how did she do that piecing?'

Heather is now starting to give away her quilts to family members, wanting to clear the decks and keep moving in new directions. All power to her prosthetic thimble. ∎

Malcolm Harrison

HE IS THE MAN WHO PIONEERED QUILTING AS AN ART FORM IN NEW ZEALAND.
MALCOLM HARRISON, THE INAUGURAL WINNER OF NEW ZEALAND'S BIGGEST
CRAFT AWARD, THE CREATIVE NEW ZEALAND CRAFT AND OBJECT ART
FELLOWSHIP, IS A STORYTELLER PAR EXCELLENCE WHO CREATES HIS
NARRATIVES IN STITCH.

The Killing Shed
draws on Canterbury farm buildings

alcolm's collection of 35 dolls, called simply *The Family*, has drawn huge numbers to galleries since it was first shown at The Dowse in 1987. *These are Matters of Pride —* the largest public artwork commissioned in New Zealand — and the wall hanging *Whanaungatanga* (Relationships) are also seen by thousands of visitors to Parliament House each year.

Malcolm Harrison was working as a Christchurch window dresser when he emerged as a textile artist. In 1962, he won second prize in the New Zealand Gown of the Year award, a fairy tale fashion extravaganza that wowed the country from 1958 to 1964, for *Scheherazade* — an understated, strapless evening gown in olive delustred satin with pearl- and sequin-encrusted crewelwork embroidery — and his work continued to feature during the show's brief history.

These days his work is held in public and private collections throughout New Zealand, Australia and the US. The Dowse, in Lower Hutt, has held several major exhibitions of his

Inspired by poet Tomas Transtromer's 'Each man is a half open door leading to a room for everyone', Malcolm sheds light on hitherto closed spaces — and in honouring his dad, creates his own memoir.

sometimes huge quilts, and in 2005, Te Papa bought a large stitched work for its collection.

Now resident on Waiheke Island, Malcolm moved to Wellington from Bayswater, Auckland in 1994 to work on the design and creation of two works for the refurbished Galleria area of Parliament. Co-ordinating the efforts of over 700 embroiderers from 52 guilds around the country, and four Maori weavers, was bound to be difficult at times. His reflections on the often fraught process of dealing with bureaucracy

emerged in the 1997 exhibition 'Exquisite Mysteries', nineteen small, richly coloured and symbol-laden needlepoint works with such titles as *The House is Sitting* and *It Looks Like Upside-Down To Me*.

Malcolm has the knack of making new beginnings — every project involves a clean sweep in many ways, from the research stage to completion. *Just Another Year*, a series on the four seasons stitched while he was in the capital, is now in Te Manawa's collection, in Palmerston

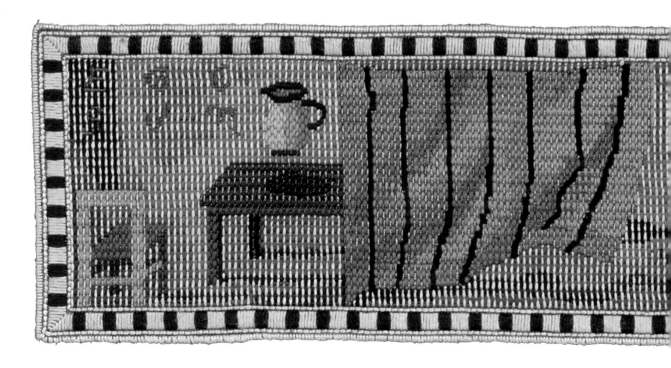

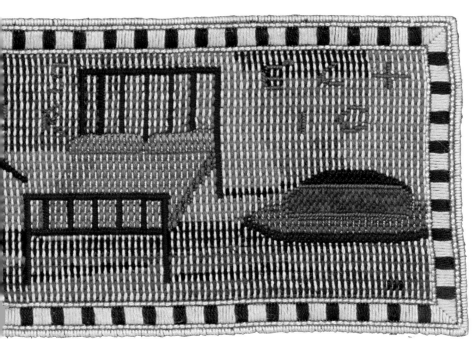

Malcolm Harrison with his linen and felt work inspired by a Papua New Guinean mud-painted mat

The Big Cheese *is a political work about hospital reform*

North. Returning to Auckland, it struck him just how much he had missed the harbour and Hauraki Gulf. He expressed his feelings in simple stitched works hinting at baches, boats and beacons as well as the light, the night, the rain — elements that endure, always — hence the title *Sempre*.

In *Open and Closed Spaces*, first shown at Te Manawa in 2005 before touring, Malcolm recalls his father Jim Harrison — a builder to whom he first paid tribute after his death in 1981, in a series of white quilts. Inspired by poet Tomas Transtromer's 'Each man is a half open door leading to a room for everyone', Malcolm sheds light on hitherto closed spaces — and in honouring his dad, creates his own memoir. Eighteen eloquent and deceptively simple works, with titles such as *Dwang*, *Scaffolding* and *A builder's pencil*, use quilting, canvas work and stem stitch to create a symbol-laden narrative that evokes his childhood. Buildings are a metaphor for life, bird wings for inner freedom; and Jim's dog is there too, his 'mad as hell' spaniel Ted.

The award of the Creative New Zealand fellowship in June 2004 at last gave Malcolm the time and resources to focus on creating his own art. He says receiving the $65,000 fellowship allowed him to continue pushing the boundaries of his work. 'Once you get on a roll it just keeps getting bigger. With the resources to do the job, you can keep on that roll.' The work that came out of that year, shown at Objectspace in Ponsonby, was called *Minus Reason*. Triggered by Francisco Goya's famous etching *The Dream of Reason Produces Monsters*, which shows an artist sleeping at his desk surrounded by spooky creatures of the imagination, Malcolm's installation was created in response to recent events in Afghanistan and Iraq.

His latest work goes back to a period spent in Papua New Guinea in the sixties, when he bought a woven mat patterned with pink and white clay and soot. Clearing out a basement recently, he rediscovered the treasure and has made two interpretations in felt, which were shown at NorthArt, Northcote, in September 2006.

Malcolm says he will probably continue to live on Waiheke, where the seascape has a very strong pull. 'The sheer amount of water and sky, the way the wind skips across the water, the way the light skips across the water. Every little ripple picks up the sun, it's like looking into a whole sheet of lurex.' ■

'Once you get on a roll it just keeps getting bigger. With the resources to do the job, you can keep on that roll.'

LEFT: *This work is about the senses — touch, hearing, sight and taste*

ABOVE: Day of the Equinox *is an interpretation of Giotto's mural* The Last Judgement, *which is in the Scrovegni Chapel in Padua, Italy.*

Susan Holmes

IN NEW ZEALAND, THE NAME SUSAN HOLMES HAS
BECOME SYNONYMOUS WITH WEARABLE ART. HER ABILITY
TO TRANSFORM FABRIC INTO FLUID REPRESENTATIONS OF
FANTASTICAL CREATURES IS LEGENDARY. YET THE REAL
PERSON IS HUMBLE, UNPRETENTIOUS AND GENEROUS TO
HER FELLOW PRACTITIONERS.

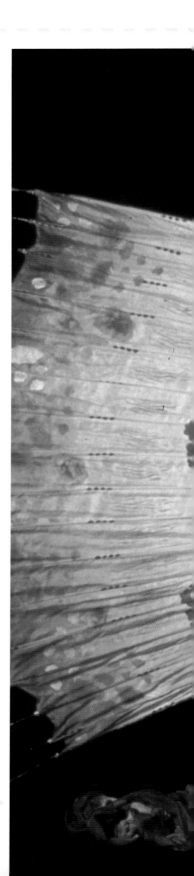

t here can't be many New Zealanders
who wouldn't recognise the wearable
artwork of Susan Holmes. Her
dramatic, hand-dyed silk and tapered
cane *Dragon Fish* (pictured right), winner of the
Supreme Award in 1996, has become an emblem
of the annual WOW (World of Wearable Arts)
show, summing up the whole elaborate and
over-the-top nature of the event. The stuff of
fable, her creation has elements of both fish and
dragon, the mythic and marine, with a groper-
like mouth that could conceivably breathe fire.
Every move the model makes emphasises the
supple beauty of the winged form.

Commenting on her award, judge Gary
Mackay said it was obvious from the beginning
that the garment was a winner. 'We all gasped
when we saw it. It's not just pretty, it's beautiful.'

Dragon Fish *has become
synonymous with the annual
World of Wearable Art event.*

The hand-dyed silk work, now in the permanent exhibition at the WOW museum in Nelson, took just three weeks to make — astonishing when you consider that some artists' entries take much of the year to assemble.

Susan's kimono-inspired *Blue Lagoon* (pictured below), a fluid, dyed nylon representation of the traditional Japanese garment, was runner-up — and undoubted audience favourite, according to sources who attended — in WOW 2003's inaugural Creative New Zealand award for Artistic Excellence, which showcases works by previous Supreme Award winners and judges. The following year, Susan took the top prize in the same category with *Miro Personage*, a witty embodiment of one of her favourite artist's best-known images, interpreting the theme 'From impressionism to surrealism'.

In 2005, Susan was runner-up again with a very different look indeed — the simple, all-white *Cage of Thorns* (opposite), a corset and skirt of eleagnus wands, cotton and linen. She chose eleagnus because it is very supple and strong, 'pliable and not too prickly, although it looks it!' Susan was intrigued by the dual nature of protection and threat implied in the garment. 'It

The kimono-inspired Blue Lagoon *is made of dyed nylon.*

is a cage and it limits the wearer yet it strangely supports and emphasises the body shape,' she says. 'The body has protection in the form of a corset. It's a mixture of things all happening at once.'

Susan began entering and garnering awards from her earliest fabric art days — the Benson and Hedges Fashion Awards in the seventies, the Mohair awards in the eighties — before wearable art took over. Yet, unlike most textile artists, sewing was not her first love.

The Auckland-born artist has a Master of Home Science degree from Otago where, in pre-feminist days, she was considered very daring for riding a motorbike. Her Masters thesis was in nutrition, not textiles.

At undergraduate level, students were expected to do everything, but while textile chemistry was a specialist subject, sewing itself was not one of her favourites.

'I was hopeless at it,' she says, 'cack-handed, rough and ready, and I didn't take it at all seriously. I really came to it by accident, when I couldn't sell my fabric printing unless I made it up into garments'.

As well as taking part in group and solo exhibitions for many years, Susan has completed commissions for large works such as the 17-metre-wide spinnaker cloth banners in the Chase Plaza building in Auckland. Like a handful of other top textile artists, she has also contributed behind the scenes to the highly successful television series *Hercules* and *Xena, Warrior Princess*.

Underpinning Susan's successes are years of experience in fabric printing and dyeing. Rudimentary potato block prints patterned the earliest of the thousands of hand-dyed and printed dresses she sold, over a decade or so from 1971, at the Auckland craft co-operative Brown's Mill. The public flocked every weekend to the Mill, Auckland's original craft market, where Susan and Valerie Hunton were the only people selling hand-dyed and printed silk garments.

In those years, while she was raising her three children, Susan lived and worked at the Centrepoint Community in Albany, north of Auckland.

Recently, she has been making more fashion garments, which have always been for the higher end of the market. Many have become heirlooms, handed down from mother to daughter. Earlier couture pieces are also finding their way into museum collections — Auckland Museum's textile collection now has around ten pieces, including three wearable art garments, and Warkworth's Parry Kauri Museum, which has an extensive textile collection, includes a peachy handpainted and dyed ensemble. The World of Wearable Art in Nelson now owns 23 Susan Holmes pieces.

Looking back, Susan says no matter what has been happening in the rest of her life, her fabric art has always been at the centre. 'I'm just so lucky to have been able to work with art and textiles.' ▰

LEFT: Cage of Thorns *'limits the wearer yet strangely supports and emphasises the body shape'.*

Laura Hudson

LAURA HUDSON'S TEXTILE WORK REFLECTS HER 'LIFELONG BATTLE WITH DOMESTICITY'. IN 2000, SHE ADDED A DEGREE IN PRINTMAKING TO HER COMPREHENSIVE BACKGROUND IN EMBROIDERY, SO AS TO BETTER EXPRESS HER IDEAS ABOUT WOMEN AND THEIR WORK.

Seasonal Adjustments
uses appliqué and piecing to play with form and colour.

ow do women learn their roles? Where do we get our ideas of femininity from?

Laura Hudson believes it is mostly from our mothers, just as they learned from their mothers. 'Homework', her 2004 exhibition at Palmerston North's Te Manawa, combined embroidery, lace, buttons and patchwork with prints on cloth in order to demonstrate aspects of women's lives on the home front — and how they have changed. The most dramatic piece was the train, modelled on a wedding gown. Around 5 metres long and 1.5 metres wide (at its widest point) it incorporates buttons, screenprinting and patchwork on cotton damask, the stuff of tablecloths. Like *In Service Training* (page 111), with its 'pinnies', it involved Laura in the 'meditative act' of sewing on thousands of buttons by hand.

'My mother made keeping house look simple,' she says in her introduction to 'Homework', 'but when it was my turn I discovered that the endless repetition of small tasks is the sort of work that is only noticed by its absence'. As she notes, you never remark on how

'I am not a purist where technique is concerned. If it fits the concept I am engaged with, I'll use it.'

well-dusted a house looks — only on the fact that it has not been dusted.

Laura chooses to celebrate, rather than denigrate, the selflessness of routine and repetitive tasks that contributed historically to the order and pleasure of the home. She pays tribute to the urge to beautify with whatever means come to hand.

Laura has had a peripatetic life. Born in Eritrea, at that time part of Ethiopia, where her father was an army doctor, she moved with her family to Britain as a two-year-old. Searching for a way to express herself as a young adult, she trained to become a drama teacher. Along the way she discovered stage design, in which she graduated with distinction. However, after six months of theatre life in the provinces she discovered she didn't love stage design enough to put up with other aspects of theatre life — 'and crucially, I lacked the confidence to push myself in that world'.

Later she completed Part I of the City and Guilds creative embroidery course at the Chelsea School of Art, under Betty Myerscough, who taught her the importance of technique as a means to an end, rather than an end in itself — of realising the creative idea, rather than presenting a distraction for the viewer. 'It had a huge influence on me,' Laura says. 'I had three years with her and still like to use whatever technique that is to hand that will further the interests of the moment.'

While living in Jamaica in the eighties with her husband, a maths professor, and their children, Laura exhibited her work and lectured part-time in layered and stitched textiles at the Jamaica School of Art, now the Edna Manley School for the Visual Arts. This was a very stimulating environment which included some of the best artists on the island.

In 1987, Laura came to New Zealand with her family. In 1992 and 1993, she was selected for inclusion in the ten-day Queen Elizabeth II Arts Council-funded Stitched Textile Design Symposia, facilitated by Carole Shepheard. It was 'one of those fairy tale moments' for Laura. 'It changed the way I thought about doing things. Since working at the Jamaica School of Art, I had been conscious of wanting to make my work more meaningful in some way. The challenges and encouragement of people like Carole Shepheard, Malcolm Harrison, Emma Robertson and Michael Brennand-Wood all helped me move in this direction.' Work by symposia participants was exhibited at the Barbican Arts Centre in London in 1996 and later toured New Zealand.

Laura's machine-embroidery skills were employed on the *Sea Panel* of Malcolm Harrison's Galleria project for Parliament. Her designs, based on marine life forms, were selected and approved by Malcolm and machine-embroidered white on white. 'It provided textural interest only, as it was painted and

In Service Training *uses cloth printed with the images of women from Laura Hudson's family, and thousands of handsewn buttons.*

printed over.'

In 1992, she made a commissioned work for Palmerston North City Council, 2.4 metres long and 1 metre wide, called *Manawatu: river and sky*, which hung in the council offices for thirteen years.

Laura turned to printmaking in 1998, building her own etching press as part of her degree at Whanganui Polytechnic's Quay School of the Arts. She went on to lecture in printmaking at UCOL@Wairarapa and was a temporary lecturer in printmaking at Massey University's College of Education.

Laura alternates her work exploring issues of gender role formation with more formal issues of colour and composition, in pieced and appliquéd quilts such as *Seasonal Adjustments* (page 108). 'I am not a purist where technique is concerned,' she says. 'If it fits the concept I am engaged with, I'll use it.' ■

Janice Jones

THREADS HELD TOGETHER BY THE
LIGHTEST OF LINKS DISTINGUISH JANICE
JONES' TEXTILES — DIAPHANOUS, WISPY,
CREATIONS THAT ARE BARELY THERE, FANCY
YARNS, RIBBONS AND LACE HOLDING HANDS.

these fibre creations may look knitted, but in fact everything is machine-made — as in sewing machine. Janice has made the Solvy technique her own, stitching threads onto a soluble base fabric (Solvy), often in a grid or scribble pattern, then washing the base fabric away to leave a tracery of thread. To stitch the threads down she uses glitzy rayon, metallic, viscose or polyester Madeira threads — 'anything but cotton' — and no fancy stitches. The resulting fabrics are surprisingly durable.

Janice says that whenever she's travelling she can't resist an op-shop, any sort of wool shop or even a little craft shop. 'It doesn't matter if it's old, I'll poke around for the things that people

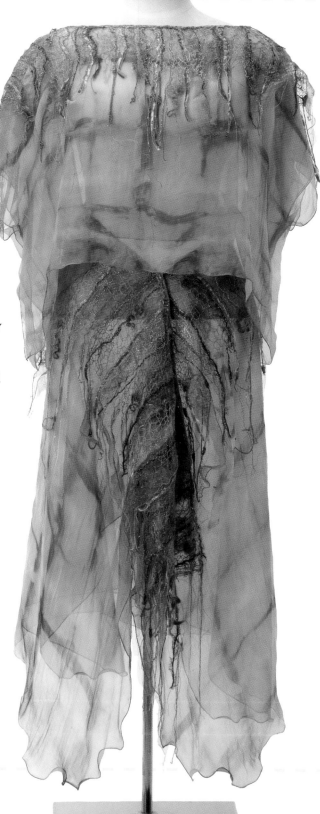

Layers of thread are held together with machine stitching in Janice Jones' diaphanous dresses. Water Nymph, *left, was a finalist in the Creative Fibre Festival, 2005.*

don't buy, that nobody wants.' She loves bead shops, and looks out for interesting yarns to make pompoms and tassels. Even coloured safety pins suit her purpose. She needs lots of thread, silk slivers, nets, beads, feathers and leathers to make her shawls, scarves, vests and the occasional whole garment.

Janice and her husband Carrick had a dress fabric and haberdashery shop, Jones of Wanaka, for many years, finally leaving it in 1998. When the demand for patchwork fabric began, Janice decided she should see what it was all about. 'That was the beginning and end of it,' she says. 'It blew my mind. I wanted to do it all, wanted to know all about it. I've been working overtime ever since, going to lots of classes and workshops — all kinds.'

Janice would like to have made art quilts — she has won a good handful of awards for her patchwork and attended every national symposium since she took it up — but she gravitates towards the kind of clothing she and Carrick had in the shop, which she left eight years ago to work fulltime on her textiles. 'I could see that I could make that, so I started. But

A light-as-air scarf using the wash-away Solvy base fabric.

'I like the idea of Creative Fibre and I like to enter exhibitions and symposiums — it's an indication of how your work is going and how the standards are set.'

I never could associate patchwork with clothing. I used some of the techniques and more and more embellishment instead.'

A Wanaka Autumn Art School class in the Solvy technique, with Australian Glenys Mann, made Janice realise she could do something with the product. She started entering the annual Creative Fibre fashion awards in 2003 and has never looked back, winning two awards each year. 'The next year I had to keep going, to see if I could do it again.' In 2004, her long hooded sleeveless coat *Cardrona Spirit* won the Sheer Fashion award and the award for the most outstanding garment. *Water Nymph* (page 112) was a finalist in the Accent Fibres award in the 2005 Creative Fibre Festival.

She has entered every year except 2006, when the arrival of her first two grandbabies saw a change in priorities. 'I like the idea of Creative Fibre and I like to enter exhibitions and symposiums — it's an indication of how your work is going and how the standards are set.'

She is currently planning a hanging for an arched doorway in an American house, using the colours of the landscape — tussock, grasses, flaxes, all quite neutral — having previously made two hangings for the same client's Wanaka home. 'He likes the idea of being able to see through it, without it blocking any views — the translucency of it.' Both Janice and her client are 'absolutely delighted' with the way the hangings have performed, with no wear and tear showing on the softly draping wool and wool-sliver fabric. A little bit of glitter reflects light, creating an effect like dew on the grasses. The hangings are quite long and swathe onto the floor, so they still touch the ground when tied to one side.

'A commission is a challenge, interpreting what the person wants you to do, what colours and looks might be right. We took photos of views, flaxes and grasses, plants, the stone floor. I made up a booklet of about 50 textures and yarns so I can go back to it.'

This is something Janice has made a practice of, since every work is different. She writes down all the details, collects samples of yarns, threads and embellishments, and takes photos. 'I could never do one exactly the same though.' ∎

Laurel Judd

LAUREL JUDD HAD A GO AT JUST ABOUT EVERYTHING IN THE
WOOLCRAFTS LINE, FROM MACRAMÉ TO CROCHET, BEFORE FINDING HER
REAL PASSION — MACHINE KNITTING. BUT SHE DOESN'T JUST LIMIT
HERSELF TO GARMENTS, TURNING HER HAND TO WALL HANGINGS AND
THREE-DIMENSIONAL SCULPTURE AS WELL.

 Spinning and weaving were way
too slow for this former dancer,
gymnast and athlete turned high
school physical education teacher.
Having to fit her textile crafts into time left
over from teaching, plus raising a family of two,
meant the quicker the production, the more she
could achieve.

Crochet was quicker than handspinning,
and she even made some money from that.
Dresses for herself, her friends and their
friends; bedspreads; her own wedding dress,
including coat, train and hood, and dresses for
her three bridesmaids.

Then it was macramé, tying everyone in
knots in the school staffroom at lunchtime,
with metres of string. 'I went all out at it and
made macramé bags and belts and hangings for
everyone I knew and took orders too.'

She had been aware of knitting machines, as
her mother had one for a while. Laurel would
come home from school in the afternoon to find
another jersey completed. So, recently married
and in her early twenties, she decided to buy a
knitting machine — and she was away.

By now Laurel was teaching, but in the
school holidays she went back every day for more
free knitting lessons. With the technology to
match her creative flow, Laurel at last had a way
of speedily producing metres of knitted wool,
similar to the ropes of French knitting she and
her brother had wrapped around the house when
they were little. These days her machine-knitted
versions of those cords dangle from the bottom
of kids' garments, decorate dressed-up chairs
and insinuate their way across evening capes.

The woman who launched herself into
machine-knitting full-time ten years ago and

'Contact your local club — the members may be getting on in years but they have a huge amount of knowledge to offer. Get into it!'

Split Enz in Repose
— *a machine knitted tribute to New Zealand's most famous band by Laurel Judd, opposite in her Taradale studio.*

set up her own business, Laurel Dzigna Knitz, also began entering design competitions; as she puts it, 'They offer an excuse to create something really special'. Inspiration comes from just about everywhere — fashion magazines, calendars, greeting cards, her garden, and the views from the house and studio, designed by her architect husband Tim and tucked into the Taradale hills.

Rosettes and ribbons decking the walls of her studio include the top prizes from every possible exhibition, from the Machine Knitters of New Zealand to Opotiki Fleece and Fibre, Creative Fibre Fashion Awards, the Alpaca Association's New Zealand Fibre Expo and the finals of the Norsewear Art Awards. She made the finals of

the Benson and Hedges Fashion Design Awards too, stood next to judge Imran Khan, then saw her garment worn back-to-front on the catwalk!

As well as the standard handcrafted, fully fashioned garments like jackets, jumpers, dresses, leggings and accessories, Laurel uses her three machines to create fabric for use in lieu of rag strips in rugs, multi-patterned samples in wall hangings, fine knit to create wedding dresses and pieces for appliqué. Although she could incorporate some designs into the pattern — and much of this can now be done on computer and downloaded to the knitting machine — she prefers using appliqué, embroidery, felting, beading and other embellishing techniques 'to give a bolder line'. She loves to incorporate other craft techniques with her knitting to produce distinctive pieces for fashion and works of art.

She will often run up a 'toile' from knit fabric to try out a garment shape before adapting it for her machine, because every stitch must be accounted for. She will knit fabric then felt it in her washing machine; she'll weave whole garments by laying rows of yarn or sliver across the bed of the knitting machine by hand. Any fibre pliable enough to put through her machine gets a chance, from the thickest bouclés to metallic yarns, and including some that have to be hand-manipulated. One fabric, made (very slowly) from fine-gauge wire and variegated sewing machine thread, offered new possibilities in terms of moulding and shaping. Even jewellery is possible. 'There are just so many things to explore!'

Split Enz in Repose (opposite page) took the top award at the Hawke's Bay Review, a forum for all arts and crafts by locals, in 2004. The work, one of several chairs Laurel has made that you can really sit in, recalls those crazy suits the band wore in their heyday, with stripes, spots, zigzag checks and bead-trimmed fringe on an asymmetric club chair shape, finished off with loopy yellow 'French knitting' scallops. Another chair has a seat entirely covered in pompoms.

Today, Laurel has an international reputation as a judge and tutor, has written four instructional books and created numerous patterns for international machine knitting magazines. She is relentless in her crusade for machine knitting to be recognised as an art form — after all, she points out, spinners have their wheels, weavers their looms and quilters their sewing machines. Laurel is also passionate about sharing the skills of her craft and loves to tutor machine knitting and creative fibre techniques.

Laurel continues to sell directly from her home studio where she displays her art works and a wide range of ready to wear fashion garments. She also offers a made-to-measure service for special occasion wear and original designs. ▪

Like the weavers of old, Heeni Kerekere is constantly trying new things, such as this work made from harakeke (New Zealand flax) pods.

Heeni Kerekere

ONE OF ONLY A HANDFUL OF WEAVERS TAKING TRADITIONAL SKILLS INTO THE CONTEMPORARY ARENA, HEENI KEREKERE IS STILL TEACHING RARANGA, OR TRADITIONAL WEAVING. SHE LEARNED TO WEAVE FLAX IN EARLY 1980 AND HASN'T STOPPED SINCE.

eeni says that in the old days when weavers were working at their craft, they were the contemporary artists of their time. 'They were constantly creating, constantly trying new things. That is all I am trying to do.' A weaver, painter and clayworker of Te Whanau-a-Apanui, Te Aitanga-a-Mahaki and Kai Tahu descent, Heeni has used harakeke (New Zealand flax) pods in five pieces so far and is still developing that idea.

A cloak in the British Museum, covered in clay, inspired Heeni to produce *Te Kete a Papatuanuku* (page 123) from the *Earth Basket* series, coloured with that very old dyestuff, mud. Charcoal, white clay, red earth and paru, the black mud of swamps, were used to dye textiles in pre-European days; this red kokowai clay came from a source in Northland that was pointed out to Heeni by clay worker Manos Nathan.

Traditionally, the clay — which is dried and ground before use — was quite sacred.

Heeni learned to weave in the eighties, taking advantage of one of the proliferation of government arts and crafts courses and signing up at Kokiri Marae in Seaview, Wellington. Under the tutelage of master weaver Erenora Puketapu-Hetet, she learned all the traditional uses of flax — whariki (mats), tukutuku (panels), piupiu (skirts), taniko (belts) and korowai (cloaks) — as well as how to grow, harvest, dye and conserve flax.

After a two-year training course Heeni started teaching, while continuing to learn. She moved to the north of the South Island to work on marae-based programmes at Waikawa in Picton and Whakatu in Nelson, refurbishing meeting houses as part of the learning process.

In 1990, Heeni went back to Gisborne, her home town, to Toihoukura, the visual arts department of Tairawhiti Polytechnic, where she continued to combine teaching and learning. It was co-ordinator Sandy Adsett who

'They were constantly creating, constantly trying new things.
That is all I am trying to do.'

convinced her to stick with weaving in the face of other temptations such as claywork. While at Toihoukura, she enthusiastically took up the opportunity to travel overseas — 'awesome opportunities' that included trips to Europe, China, Pacific Islands, and places such as Santa Fe and Phoenix in the US, where she saw the work done by some of the native American tribes. A trip to Seattle gave her the opportunity to demonstrate weaving in association with the touring exhibition 'Toi Maori: The Eternal Thread'.

In 1996, Heeni was awarded Gisborne Museum of Art and History's Ruanuku Art Award in recognition of her skills as a leading fibre artist and as Toihoukura's most innovative student artist that year. Two years later she opened an art gallery and shop in Gisborne with five friends and family members. The gallery, called Ukaipo, is also the venue for monthly exhibitions and wananga. A grant from Te Waka Toi, the Maori arts council, helped her take her whariki wananga to other areas over three years, refurbishing marae in the process.

Over her 25 years as a teacher, Heeni has continued her own training as well as sharing her skills with students of all ages in many environments — at Arohata Prison and Epuni Boys' Home, with at-risk and special-needs students in Gisborne, and at marae-based courses, polytechnics and wananga from Wainuiomata to Gisborne and Tauranga.

Her projects have included the refurbishment of Hinetamatea Marae at Anaura Bay, north of Gisborne. She also helped decorate Te Tumu Herenga Waka, the wharenui (meeting house) at Victoria University, where to satisfy fire regulations the tukutuku panels were woven from kangaroo-hide strips, in spite of demonstrating that traditional flax lit up quickly then went out, whereas the kangaroo hide kept burning. 'It was still a beautiful effect,' she says, 'and there was not a lot of preparation, which was good'.

Since moving to Huntly in order to teach at Te Wananga o Aotearoa in Hamilton, Heeni has gone back to making kete. She would like to weave large wall pieces, but without the machinery available at her previous workplace at Toihoukura, which allowed her to work wood to mix with her fibre, she is staying small.

After working as a teacher, Heeni would now like to do something for herself. There's a whole tradition to explore in the use of mud dyes, and

she is keen to try her hand at weaving kareao, or
supplejack, which was traditionally used to make
hinaki or eel traps. But there are very few people
to bounce ideas off — she loves the work of
master weavers Toi Maihi and Maureen Lander,
but 'can't get enough of it'. So Heeni will have to
continue to draw her inspiration from nature. ▪

*Inspired by a cloak in
the British Museum, Te
Kete a Papatuanuku
(The Earth Mother's
Basket) is coloured with
red clay.*

Ming Wei Li

DESCRIBED BY LECTURERS AS ONE
OF THE MOST TALENTED FASHION
DESIGNERS TO COME THROUGH
MASSEY UNIVERSITY IN THE LAST
20 YEARS, MING WEI LI WAS
AWARDED THE ULTIMATE ACCOLADE
BY HIS CLASSMATES IN 2005, WHO
DECIDED UNANIMOUSLY TO GIVE
HIM THE HONOUR OF SHOWING HIS
GARMENTS AS THE FINALE OF THEIR
CATWALK GRADUATION SHOW,
'HEMS TO THE LEFT'.

One of Ming Wei Li's
Modern Opera
*collection, based on Beijing
Opera costumes.*

Pushing creative boundaries has become something of an overused cliché, but Ming Wei gathered a reputation at Massey for his exceptional ability at picking up new techniques to produce exciting work. Fashion design lecturer, Vince Beckett, says Ming is certainly one of the most talented students he has been associated with in his 20 years at the college.

Born in 1979, in Wei Hai city in China's southern Shan Dong province, Ming came to New Zealand with his parents and older brother in 2000 so he could continue his study of fashion design, begun at Shan Dong's Technology and Art University. Four years later, he graduated from Massey in Wellington with honours and took the award for Creative Flair.

Always drawing as a child, Ming was encouraged by his mother, an importer of South Korean clothing and fabric, to learn piano from the age of seven. In his teens he studied art. 'My mother supported me a lot,' he says. 'She always wanted me to learn something in the artistic and musical area.'

But it was seeing British fashion designer John Galliano's work in a magazine that made

'I think New Zealand fashion is rising up very fast,' he says. 'I am not sure what it will look like in a few years. But I will start my brand in New Zealand if it seems possible.'

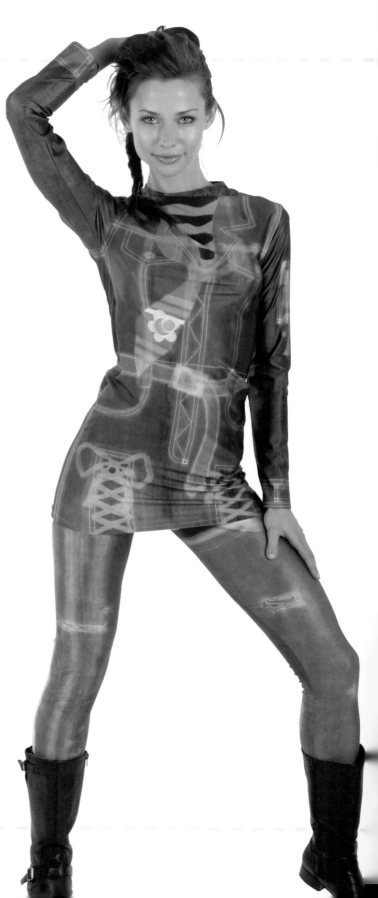

him want to study fashion. 'His works are amazing,' says Ming. 'He became my favourite designer, so I decided I too wanted to design something beautiful, amazing, interesting but not too commercial. I love doing craft works as well.'

Ming was a runner-up in the national Lycra student fashion design awards for two years running, and his 2005 *trompe l'oeil* printed *Date in Double Denim* (pictured right) streetwear garment — looking like a jacket, tie and torn jeans — could well have been body-painted onto his model.

But it was his powerful and dynamic graduating collection of six garments, entitled *Modern Opera*, and marked by stunning colour and playful pattern, that truly set him apart at graduation. Based on Chinese traditional garments and the facemasks of what used to be called Peking Opera — now Beijing Opera — Ming's collection exploits the strong colour contrast that marks the tradition's costumes. He concentrated on modernising the designs, colours and shapes of the garments; printed his own fabric, constructed tailored garments and decorated them with flourishes of machine-knitted and hand-crocheted details.

Although he is constantly pushing the

LEFT: **Date in Double Denim** *is a two-piece Lycra garment that could have been body-painted on to the model*

RIGHT: *A knitting machine was used to make a sweater without seams — a tubular sleeve and body, with three scarves at the neck.*

creative boundaries, Ming is still a strong believer in tradition. He says using its style on modern garments creates a balance between the old and the new. 'Tradition will never be forgotten because it will continue to inspire modern fashion designers. When married with modern fashion it reflects its origin and classical nature but also endows the garments with an extraordinarily fresh meaning.'

His target customer, he says, is likely to be young and rich. 'She would like to party, go to clubs and be the centre of attention. She would probably live in Europe, North America or Japan.'

While currently working in Auckland, it is easy to imagine Ming being snapped up by some overseas fashion house before too long. Inquisitive and ambitious, he is not afraid to take big risks and he has the talent to pull them off. Once he has enough pattern making or designing experience he wants to launch his own brand. With any luck, it will be in New Zealand. 'I think New Zealand fashion is rising up very fast,' he says. 'I am not sure what it will look like in a few years. But I will start my brand in New Zealand if it seems possible.' ∎

Robin McLaughlin

FINE WEAVING HAS REMAINED AT
THE CORE OF ROBIN MCLAUGHLIN'S
PRACTICE, SOME THREE DECADES
AFTER SHE FIRST TOOK LESSONS
FROM A TRADITIONAL NEW
ENGLAND WEAVER IN BOSTON,
MASSACHUSETTS.

n 2006, Robin created an heirloom, a finely woven christening gown for her first grandchild, Felix. Made of fine merino wool, with silk woven across it for softness and lustre, it has a fine stripe of blue, red and gold down one side — just to make it a bit different.

A Home Science graduate of Otago University, Robin later completed a Masters degree in Food Science in Tennessee. However,

Painted warps add abstract and very random colour interest to Robin McLaughlin's collapsed weave scarves.

it was in Boston, while her husband Charles was on a post-doctoral fellowship at Massachusetts General Hospital, associated with Harvard University, that she finally seized the opportunity to learn to weave.

Robin had been an embroiderer for many years but couldn't easily find threads for her work. Night classes were her introduction to the very traditional, New England style of weaving fine cotton yarn in traditional overshot patterns — the patterns used for fine American linen and, in larger sizes, for woven coverlets. It was a natural progression from the pulled-thread and counted-thread needlework that Robin loved.

Growing up in Winton, Southland, in a family of handcrafters — 'Grandmother made socks, Mother did smocking, everybody was doing something' — Robin had a basic understanding of textiles. Although Home Science included courses in design, textile

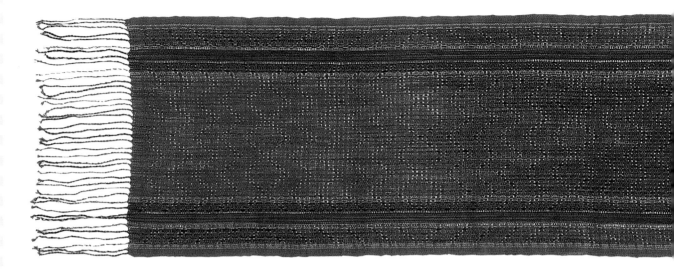

A scarf echoing the traditional American huck lace patterns that were Robin McLaughlin's introduction to weaving in New England.

'The use of fine threads in scarves, wraps, fabrics and linens, plus the opportunity to incorporate needlework with handwoven linen, remains my main weaving interest.'

science and clothing, she didn't really do craft work until after graduation, when she joined the staff of the school and had more time for creative activity. The design department was just starting to offer pottery and weaving, and she can still remember when a friend and colleague brought home one of the school's rigid-heddle looms and they tried to figure out how it worked using handspun wool.

Robin bought her first loom, a table loom, in 1980. These days, she has two eight-shaft countermarche looms, made by Mecchia Looms in Hamilton, (at her home in Dunedin's North East Valley). One has a dobby mechanism, which Robin describes as 'one step before computerisation — it works a bit like an old punch-card machine, using lags and pegs rather than cards with holes'. She sets up the pattern sequences before she starts weaving, then has to use only two pedals, rather than the ten on the other loom. 'It's ideal for complex weaves with long repeating pattern sequences.'

In 1997, Robin bought the business of

Glenora Craft from Picton weaver Birgite Armstrong, and moved it to Dunedin. She imports and sells yarns, dyes and equipment. She finds this a wonderful way to maintain contact with other weavers — as well as access to a stock of yarns for her own weaving. 'The choice this offers has greatly increased my interest in the use of a range of yarn types, singly or together, and the effect this can have on the finished product.

'I travel to woolcrafts festivals to sell the yarns, and find this a good chance to see what others are doing. I can expand my business and my ideas for weaving and whenever possible enter for the national exhibition that's held annually.'

Local gatherings are also likely to host Robin and her yarns, and weavers, spinners and embroiderers can call in, by appointment, and choose from a rainbow of yarns.

Robin enjoys painting warps to add 'abstract and very random' colour interest to her scarves and wraps — as in the collapsed weave scarves (above) — with Earth Palette dyes, which can be used cold. 'You wrap the dyed warp in plastic and keep it warm for 24 to 48 hours and then it's ready to use.' She has recently been exploring collapsed weave for her scarves, using a very fine wool crepe single yarn as the weft. 'It wants to turn in on itself — it's the energy in the yarn itself, the weave you use and the way you sett it, that collapses the yarn when the article is put into water after weaving which gives the characteristic effect,' she says.

As well as belonging to the Spinners and Weavers Guild and the Professional Weavers' Network, Robin meets each week with four or five other weavers to weave and share ideas, which she says is 'very rewarding and supportive'.

'The use of fine threads in scarves, wraps, fabrics and linens, plus the opportunity to incorporate needlework with handwoven linen, remains my main weaving interest. It is the structure of the woven cloth as well as its handle which still gives me most pleasure.' ▪

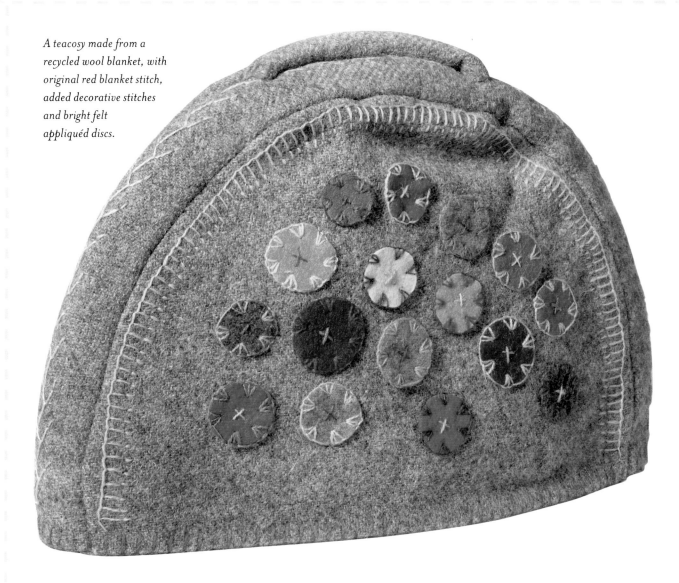

A teacosy made from a recycled wool blanket, with original red blanket stitch, added decorative stitches and bright felt appliquéd discs.

Rosemary McLeod

AN OLD SEWING BOX BOUGHT AT AUCTION STARTED WRITER, AND NOW TEXTILE ARTIST, ROSEMARY MCLEOD ON A SEARCH FOR IDENTITY — AND SOME EMBROIDERY SKILLS.

The upmarket version of the teacosy in black felt with more formal embroidery and beading.

osemary McLeod is best known as a newspaper columnist and cartoonist with an eye for the absurd, but the last few years have seen her alter ego, the passionate collector of textiles, publicly revealed. Now the veteran journalist is metamorphosing once more: her first textile works were exhibited in Wellington before Christmas 2005 — felt tea cosies at Taia Gallery in Kilbirnie — and in February 2006, a collection of 20 dolls was shown at dealer Jenny Neligan's Bowen Galleries.

'Thrift to Fantasy', the exhibition of Rosemary's collection of textile crafts from the thirties, forties and fifties was so popular that its season at The Dowse in 2002–3 was extended. Research for that exhibition culminated in a book of the same name. By then, Rosemary had started to stitch in felt, creating bags in the lighter, modern equivalent of the heavier old felts in her collection. She also began making felt and woollen tea cosies bedecked with clusters of flowers.

'Felt is just a gift for appliquérs,' she says. 'I love twenties, thirties and forties feltwork. But I love the over-the-topness of the Victorians.' So while she relishes straight appliqué, Rosemary has moved on a step further and embellished

'Maybe I wouldn't be a dollmaker if it wasn't for Malcolm. I had wanted to buy
one, but as they weren't for sale, I had to make my own.'

Eleanor Page — *seven of twenty incarnations of Rosemary McLeod's 1930s 'name in search of an identity'.*

'Felt is just a gift for appliquérs,' she says. 'I love twenties, thirties and forties feltwork. But I love the over-the-topness of the Victorians.'

the flowers with embroidery and beading. She is self-taught, using old books and the memory of historic felt work seen at London's Victoria and Albert Museum, which employed more creative techniques than she had seen before.

What Rosemary really wanted, ever since she first saw them at The Dowse, was one of Malcolm Harrison's dolls, now in the art museum's collection as a 30-strong 'Family'. 'Maybe I wouldn't be a dollmaker if it wasn't for Malcolm. I had wanted to buy one, but as they weren't for sale, I had to make my own.'

A few years ago, Rosemary bought a sewing box at an auction and uncovered a tantalising glimpse of one Eleanor Page, who was a young woman in the 1930s. There was a box of her name tags inside, and a small sheet of paper on which her mother had lovingly documented her every possible measurement for home dressmaking.

'It was a terrific name,' says Rosemary, 'a beautiful soubriquet. It should have been in romantic novels, or the debutante page. It was a name given by a mother who envisaged success on the stage, perhaps, and a future newspaper engagement notice'. It was also a name in search of an identity — a lost identity in a sewing box. It made Rosemary think about how women all sewed for their children in those days, and the whole bond and frustration of having your mother sew for you. She thought a lot about how mothers named their children, and how they knitted and sewed their identities.

This was something Rosemary never did herself — she designs her own wardrobe in collaboration with her excellent dressmaker — but she did make 'rainy day dolls' for her children, under their direction. When her youngest, Benedict, found an old book at an op-shop on how to make dolls, and said, 'You have to buy this and make me one,' they started to take shape. 'That prototype showed me a method,' she says, 'and I liked that size to work with'. There were a few portrait dolls given away as gifts, modifications to the basic pattern here and there, then manifestations of Eleanor Page began to come to life.

A Wellington dressmaker, long gone, once told her, 'If you can draw you can sew,' so Rosemary looked on the garments as problems that needed to be solved; 'drawings in fabric'. She used scraps from her vast collection of other people's leftovers and linen cupboards to make very individual representations of Eleanor — multi-racial ones too, since she had discovered during one of her past careers how much more dramatic coloured skin was than European. At first she used op-shop scraps for the doll bodies but later found a new fabric that suited her purpose.

As with her 'Thrift to Fantasy' exhibition, the Eleanor Page project grew as Rosemary stitched. Each of the 20 scarlet-lipped dolls (pages 134 and 135) is dressed to the nines — coat or costume topped by an elaborate feathered hat,

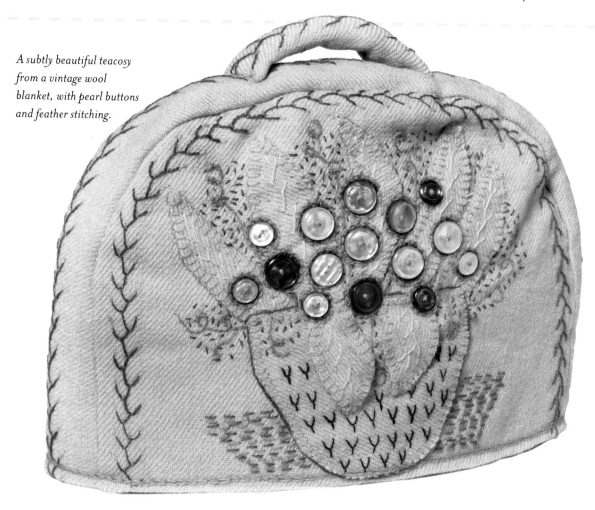

A subtly beautiful teacosy from a vintage wool blanket, with pearl buttons and feather stitching.

with handbag, jewellery, and shoes of softest kid. Most have a miniature version of the felt bags that are a personal favourite of the artist. 'And they all have underpants. I also like them to have details that aren't immediately apparent, such as lined coats or embroidery on the back of a vest which is invisible at first.'

The dolls' costumes are timeless although, interestingly, fashion has moved in this eclectic direction, Rosemary says. She has not given them names. 'I wouldn't presume to name them. I don't want to pin them down — they've got their own story. They are layered and textured in many ways and I'm not even in control of them. I like the mystery of their being nameless.' Would she like to know what became of the real Eleanor Page? 'I don't want to know! She exists in my imagination.'

The artist, who is very interested in the history of costume, sees the dolls as a kind of documentary on fashion. 'I've spent my life looking at fashion magazines,' she says. 'My name has been a newspaper byline for more years than I care to consider. I thought I could surrender this identity of mine and give it to that forgotten dream in the chest.' ∎

*Power of Red and
Yellow — a long way from
the classic nine-patch.*

Barbara McQuarrie

THIRTY-SEVEN YEARS TO THE DAY AFTER SHE STARTED HER NURSING CAREER,
BARBARA McQUARRIE DECIDED TO RETIRE FROM IT AND TAKE UP QUILTING
FULL-TIME.

t a Christchurch Hospital
reunion in September 2003
the Greymouth nurse made the
decision 'there and then' that she
had had enough of working as a general practice
nurse. Instead of nurturing her fellow humans,
she wanted to treasure and transform pieces of
special fabric, creating new works from fabrics
that have already had a life.

Barbara makes mostly small wall quilts. 'Most
people don't have big walls,' she says, 'and I have
so many ideas, I can do them faster'. Her work is
deceptively simple and instantly appealing, with
subtle colour and textural changes. She uses pure
fabrics — cotton, linen, wool, 'anything that
will take dye' — and creates interest with simple
shapes and chevron quilting reinforcing the
sometimes skewed geometry. 'I keep it simple so
the line shows.'

With a steady stream of local group
exhibitions — including some with her potter

husband Bob and daughter Caroline McQuarrie
— Barbara's biggest problem is creating a body
of work. She is currently working on nine patch
variations — or four patch with sashings. *Power of
Nine* (page 141) was inspired by a Ralph Hotere
exhibition in Christchurch, and followed by
Power of Red and Black, and *Power of Red and Yellow*.

Barbara sewed from about the age of eight,
when she made clothes for her dolls, then for
herself as a teenager, and later for her two
daughters and their dolls. Barbie dolls especially
appealed — 'All those little bits of fabric!'
Traditional patchwork came along about the
time her daughters left home, but Barbara
quickly got bored with the repetition of 'all those
blocks'. It was when she discovered it was okay
to do things without using patterns that the fun
began.

'Seven Ways to Go Crazy', a workshop by
Lynda Faires, an American woman who spent
a year in the South Island with her academic

Power of Red and Black *is another skewed nine-patch.*

'You know, when there's a problem — like when you run out of fabric — and you have to work out another way, that's what excites me.'

husband, first got Barbara excited about experimenting. Then she took a design course with Desiree Hirner, a South African-trained artist whose husband was at Grey Hospital, and started creating her own designs. Desiree became a mentor, following up after the course and pointing Barbara in the right direction. American quilter Nancy Crow's masterclass in late 2002 was the clincher — the west coaster came home from Christchurch 'very inspired'.

Much of Barbara's fabric comes from friends and family, like the three suitcases of dressmaking fabric given to her by one of her sisters. She buys very little patterned fabric but gets through a lot of plains, particularly black — 'It's quite hard to get a good black' — and she does much of her own dyeing. Men's fine wool suiting, often with subtle stripes and texture to enhance the piecing, remains a favourite.

The brown corduroy used in the quilts Barbara exhibited at te tuhi in Pakuranga, during the Auckland quilting symposium in January 2005, came from her mother-in-law's collection. 'Once upon a time I would have thrown it away,' she says, 'but it worked well with what I did'.

Her husband's mother had been a skilled sewer and a milliner, and Barbara has inherited some interesting fabrics, including 'very strange nets, little pieces of really lovely satin, and unusually wide grosgrain ribbon'. She hasn't used those pieces in her work yet, but no doubt they will make their way in eventually.

Barbara collects a lot of things that surprise her 'straight' quilting friends, although they would not look out of place in an artist's studio. She saves ends of threads, and picks out scraps from waste baskets at workshops. 'People throw out some beautiful things,' she says.

Flat West Coast beach stones have become one of Barbara's distinguishing trademarks. Reluctant to ask a friendly jade and hard-stone artist to ruin his drills making holes for her, she has found how to bind the stones before stitching them on. 'You know, when there's a problem — like when you run out of fabric — and you have to work out another way, that's what excites me,' she says. 'That's when things start happening.' ∎

ABOVE: Power of Nine *was inspired by a Ralph Hotere exhibition.*

Serena McWilliam

WHAT SERENA MCWILLIAM WOULD REALLY LOVE TO DO IS MAKE BIG SCULPTURAL PIECES OUT OF THREAD — 'BUT THAT'S A LONG WAY DOWN THE TRACK,' THE CHRISTCHURCH ARTIST ADMITS. AND SHE'LL PROBABLY NEED A LARGER SPACE THAN HER CURRENT STUDIO IN THE ARTIST'S QUARTER OF THE ARTS CENTRE.

right now Serena is working on the smaller scale creations of her *Aspiring* series, made of free-motion machine embroidery over soluble cloth (Solvy) that's dissolved away, before the resulting fabric is formed into layered conical shapes. 'I love the fact I'm building something from nothing, just thread,' she says. 'All you're left with is what you intended, nothing extra.' Different threads give different effects so Serena uses a variety, selecting for effect and resilience as appropriate. 'It gives me the option of working with it in a 2D format or using it to create sculptural pieces.'

An interest in the symbolism of plants led Serena to take up botanical drawing so she could fully understand individual plant forms before adapting them for use in either stitching or printmaking. She enjoys going on field trips with others but prefers to draw in the studio.

The spiral cones in Aspiring are built from nothing but thread, with occasional stylized leaf and flower forms.

'It was studying art history that allowed me to see the validity and potential of using stitched textiles as a contemporary art form.'

Much of her work includes plant imagery, which she finds 'a rather obliging metaphor for life'. The *Aspiring* work was developed from the sense of renewal that could be obtained by simply working in the garden. Starting by looking at the idea of unlocking, then at keys and keyhole shapes . . . 'Three notebooks later I was into spiral staircases,' she says. The work also includes occasional stylised leaf and floral forms.

Serena graduated with a Bachelor of Design (Craft) from Christchurch Polytechnic in 2003. She had grown up in a family where her mother and grandmother both stitched, but it wasn't until she was in her twenties, and living on the other side of the world, that she started to embroider.

'I was always interested in art and design, and drawn to textiles because of their tactile nature and lustrous colour — and now, increasingly, because of their history. But having been told by my art teacher that I would never get an A level in art I promptly left school and didn't actively pursue any art education until later.'

It was to be another 20 years, with her two daughters grown up, before she completed her design degree. She took lessons by correspondence while her children were small, hand-embroidering for her own enjoyment, then adult education classes at Hagley High School in design, printmaking and art history got her to Bursary level and the start of her degree. 'It was studying art history that allowed me to see the validity and potential of using stitched textiles as a contemporary art form,' she says. And although the degree course did not have a large textile component she says she did manage to get some embroidery into her sculpture option.

As a migrant, journeys, distance and the separation from family are recurrent themes — 'The way your sense of place and identity changes. They are not things you ever get out of your system,' she says.

In *The Letter* (pictured opposite), she uses part of a missive from her late great-aunt to make a poignant work in thread on paper. 'I knew the overall form I wanted it to take, but after examining the option of printing or embossing it I decided to embroider the words on the paper. That way it kept a cohesiveness.'

Driven to stitch, she nevertheless loves the research that goes into getting started on new work. 'I find it fascinating,' she says, 'but then comes the time when you do have to rein it in and actually produce something!'

Serena uses an ordinary domestic sewing machine to create her textiles. 'Because of the sort of work I do, I'm not interested in any whiz-bang effects or any of the pre-programmed stitches. What I do can be done on a very basic machine — it's like drawing with thread, only you

The Letter *is a poignant work in thread on paper, using part of a letter from Serena McWilliam's great-aunt.*

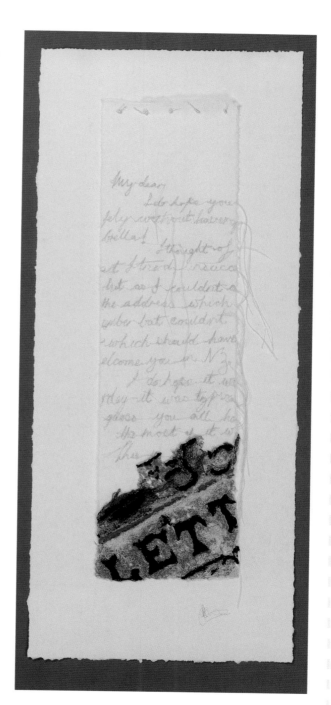

guide the support rather than the pencil, or in this case, needle.

'I like the idea that I have total control over all aspects of what's in any finished piece of work — which I guess is why I like to work on soluble fabric, where all that remains is the thread. Although there is a distinct process to go through, there's no visible residue after the process is finished. It is complete in itself, consisting of only what I choose to include — colour, motif and the degree of density or fragility.

'Also, because I work around ideas, which in themselves are abstract, I think the delicate, almost ethereal nature of the material seems appropriate. It's like working with veils of coloured light, where even slight differences in tone become visible.'

Serena's work so far has been fairly muted in colour, which she sees as appropriate for themes around memory and history. 'It's like looking back through veils. I don't think you need colour for that.' But her attitude to colour is responsive, and new work — a contemporary revisiting of Gothic revival ideas — involves rich use of colour.

Of her work Serena says: 'Although carefully crafted, there is always a concept behind the work. My intention is always to provoke some kind of response; it's never just to be looked at.' ∎

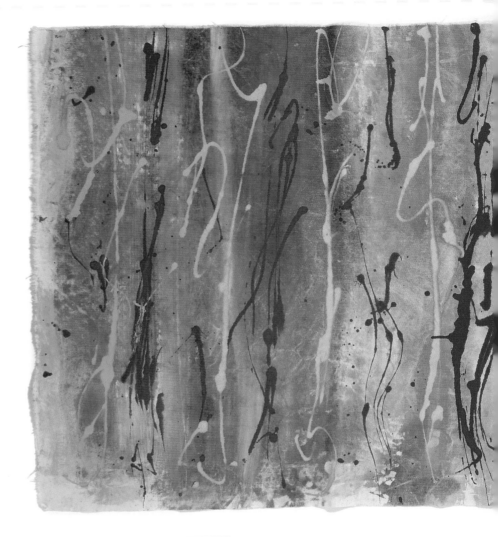

A confident hand creates upholstery fabric to live with — this for a refurbished couch in Lani Morris's Napier home.

Lani Morris

LANI MORRIS USED HER FIRST POCKET MONEY, AT THE AGE OF EIGHT, TO BUY A PIECE OF SILK. SHE HAS BEEN CREATING WITH FABRIC EVER SINCE.

now on the board of Creative Hawke's Bay, and teaching business skills at institutions such as Te Whaea, the New Zealand School of Dance and Drama in Wellington, Lani is settled back in her home town of Napier — and still working with fabric. As well as continuing to paint on silk, she is painting in oils and using house paint to create upholstery fabric that covers chairs, couches, curtains and floor rugs throughout her house.

Two disparate strands of Lani's colourful career have finally intertwined. There's the fabric artist — from tie-dyed scarves in the seventies to today's splashy upholstery fabric (pictured), via the London catwalk — and there's the training consultant with an MBA, and an MSc in Responsibility and Business Practice, who is experienced in counselling and business training, and works with a wide range of organisations.

Along the way there was also the journalist, fresh out of Canterbury University and journalism school and into recording 'Insight' radio documentaries at the age of 24; the mother; and the businesswoman, making a 'reasonable living' from her dyed and painted scarves.

The youthful craft entrepreneur was selling pottery beads and hand-painting fabric while still at Napier Girls' High School. At university she chose to do an arts degree rather than fine arts — her flatmate was doing that and Lani could

Housepaint was used to pattern these cotton duck chair coverings for restored seventies furniture.

see that weaving, her subject, was no way to make a living. She was also 'dreamy and romantic' and thought she might end up 'spending my life in the garage painting fairies and wondering why no-one bought them'.

Inspired by Fanny Buss, a Christchurch screenprinter on silk, Lani had plenty of opportunity to sell her work at markets and through shops. In an era of import restrictions, 'If you wanted something wonderful you had to make it yourself,' she says. 'A lot of craft artists started out that way.'

Her tie-dyed silk scarves sold as soon as she produced them — no one else was doing tie-dyeing then. She built up her practice during two and a half years working in broadcasting, then, burnt out by the intensity of the job she loved, left to work full-time as a fabric artist. After a year she moved to Australia, where she carried on with her work, followed by a move to London.

On the plane she saw an advertisement in *Vogue* for a London boutique called Quinquireme, and when she arrived and showed them her fabric they bought it. Some sold to fashion designer Yuki; clothes made from her fabric were being worn on the catwalk by top model Marie Helvin, with Lani looking on. 'I look back and wonder did it ever happen?' she says, but she has the programme to remind her, and the photos from *Country Life*.

When Libertys said they liked her fabric but didn't want to stock it, Lani — who now had a new baby — decided to put it all away for a while, later coming to the conclusion that what she really wanted was to do it for herself — and that was all that mattered. Back in New Zealand she started selling to shops, had a beautiful label and packaging designed, and was back in business. Her scarves were bought by the Ministry of Foreign Affairs as gifts for VIPs — there's a photo of Rosalynn Carter wearing one, and Indira Gandhi and Mrs Whitlam had them too. The business was a commercial success.

From 1979, Lani exhibited at places like the New Zealand Academy of Fine Arts and

Wellington's Turnbull House, and the Women's Gallery, which provided a space 'where I didn't have to think "I don't have a degree"'. One of their themed exhibitions was spirituality, a subject that has remained important to Lani. There was also a walk-in womb, with masses of pleated red silk. 'People disappeared inside it for hours,' she says. 'One little boy tried to charge people to come in, which struck me as very funny.' That work featured in a book by the Spiral collective on New Zealand women artists.

Lani took the top award at the Academy's ANZ Fabric and Fibre show with *Waterfall*, 180 metres of palest blue dyed silk. She dyed the same meterage for Downstage Theatre's production of *Agnes of God* — all in her washhouse in Brooklyn.

But the 1987 stockmarket crash forced a rethink and a change in direction — retraining to become a management trainer. Lani joined Wellington corporate trainers Tall Poppies and launched herself into an MBA. 'I devoured knowledge about organisations, psychology and women in management and business.'

An invitation to a Queen Elizabeth II Arts Council-funded artist workshop at Teschemakers, near Oamaru, in the nineties offered a chance to continue her art skills. Time in Australia a few years ago helped her develop her skills as a painter. Between working out in the world and spending time with her elderly mother she is creating a brilliantly coloured garden — yet another example of 'that extraordinary process of creating something from nothing' and continuing to develop new and creative approaches to business management. ■

Katherine Morrison

TO KATHERINE MORRISON THE REALISATION
THAT SHE COULD WORK WITH BLANKETS CAME
AS A KIND OF EPIPHANY.

lready notable for their
quirkiness, the Upper Hutt
stitcher's quilts took a new
direction in 2000, when she
thought about entering an Australian wool quilt
award and started looking around for fabric. 'I
bought some commercial wool fabric to make
it with but it was hard to find decent colours. It
suddenly hit me one day that I should be able to
use blankets.'

In the back of her mind somewhere there
was also the memory of quilts made from men's
woollen suiting samples, owned by an elderly
neighbour who used them to cover the garage
freezer. (These have since been exhibited at
Te Papa.) There were also the woollen wagga
coverings made during the Depression, two
of which were acquired when the Morrisons

Bed of Roses *explores
the many layers of marriage
— its intensity, fragility, joy
and sadness.*

Katherine Morrison at home in the Pinehaven bush, with a stack of salvaged blankets

bought an old bach.

Katherine, who has since made over 30 blanket quilts, has a stash of several hundred cream, grey and coloured blankets waiting for her dyepot, an old electric copper on the deck of the Morrisons' house in the bush at Pinehaven, Upper Hutt. Before the days of duvets, she says, all good Kiwis slept under woollen blankets. 'As a New Zealander, they're part of my heritage. They evoke nostalgia, frugality, austerity and comfort too. I just love them — they're warm, practical and they're very economical!'

Katherine's earliest woollen quilts exploited wool's capacity to take dyes deeply into the core of the fibre, producing textiles of intense colour — reds so saturated they throb, intense olives, brilliant golds, rich deep blues. A *Bedspring* series

captured the giant X-cross of old wirewove beds; others hinted at the ploughed paddocks of early farms, 'a calm, still, watery space behind a wire fence'.

Still packing an emotional punch, Katherine continues to explore themes close to home and hearth but the colours are more subtle, often using the op-shop sourced blankets in their original state. Stains and mends reflect human involvement, and hint at times of economic adversity in the spirit of 'make do and mend'. 'It's the worn, holey ones that I most enjoy transforming, with the idea of preserving them and giving them a sense of permanence. They can be quite beautiful or poignant in themselves.' At home, Katherine's quilts are suspended one behind the other on tensioned

'It's the worn, holey ones that I most enjoy transforming, with the idea of preserving them and giving them a sense of permanence. They can be quite beautiful or poignant in themselves.'

metal rods designed by her husband Campbell. They hang in an alcove, across the dining table from a larger-than-life portrait of Katherine, wrapped like a warrior woman in quilts, by Upper Hutt artist and friend Mary Archibald. Many of her quilts incorporate symbols lost in antiquity, including crosses and the cross-within-heart motif, an ancient symbol of lament. The crux quadrata, a very old symbol for north, south, east and west, was used in a *Dreams* series for an exhibition in 2005 at te tuhi, in Pakuranga.

Sandwiched together with simple cotton backs, embellished with a line or two of satin stitch then quilted with close running stitches, Katherine's quilts demonstrate a degree of skill in taming the thick wodge of woollen layers that few other quilters could emulate, or are even prepared to try. Yet she says it's never been a problem machine-piecing or hand-quilting the thickest woollen fabric.

In 2001, her first blanket quilt, *Fit for a Wirewove*, was a prizewinner at the biennial national quilt symposium in Queenstown, and many have garnered awards since, including, in 2004, the top prize at Pataka's biennial awards for excellence in quilting. *When Dreams Come to Visit* was a co-operative effort with artist Robert Franken, featuring his trademark haughty bird motifs, satin-stitched in light-catching lines of colour onto a classic grey blanket base.

That was a new departure for Katherine, who has since used embroidery in several series of quilts. The latest, *Bed of Roses* (page 151), which uses panels of roses in various stages to form a basic cross, was inspired by her maternal grandmother. It explores 'the many layers of marriage — its intensity, fragility, joy and sadness,' Katherine says.

'My grandmother thought marriage would be a bed of roses — and it *was* good. But in sombre contrast to her happy marriage was the Great Depression of the thirties and the horrors of World War II. At times, life was hard but Granny was the type of woman who would have comforted herself by bringing images of beauty to the forefront of her mind. I can imagine her, seeing roses on the crossbars of a window's interior, whilst in reality the exterior view was often narrow, bleak, rugged and dutiful.

'We're still primitive beings beneath our supposedly sophisticated lifestyles,' she says. 'Without warmth we die. This basic fact, plus the simple rugged form of the blanket — which has remained the same for centuries — seem to me to correspond perfectly.' ∎

Genevieve Packer

EVEN WHEN GENEVIEVE PACKER IS 'PLAYING' WITH TEXTILES, SHE'S THINKING ABOUT FUNCTIONAL PRODUCTS THAT MIGHT RESULT. 'IT'S JUST THE WAY I WORK,' SHE SAYS.

Digitally-printed fabric draws on kiwi icons such as the pohutukawa and fantails.

with other design specialities, textile design has so many different applications. 'You can dabble in a lot of them — you don't have to nail it down, and for me, no one of them outweighs the others. I get immersed in one then another. This diversity adds interest to the work, I'm not just going in any one direction.'

Craftcamp, a collaborative label sold in Wellington, has been a way of trying out new ideas. 'A fun little outlet for crafty goodness', as she calls it, craftcamp allows Genevieve to test ideas in limited editions — often using conceptual and material byproducts from other projects — without having to go into large-scale production. 'It helps me get things out of my system, to get over it quite quickly,' she says. Products made from digitally printed fabric, one of the subjects she teaches at Massey University's Wellington campus, are among craftcamp's offerings. Genevieve also teaches screen printing and textile studio papers and dabbles in web design.

The craftcamp collective, which first exhibited at Enjoy Gallery in Wellington's Cuba St, also includes Gabby O'Connor in Wellington and Shio Otani in Melbourne. Each brings a slightly different perspective to the label from her own diverse practises.

Working from a fantail theme, part of her Masters' study into images of Kiwiana, souvenirs and nostalgia, Genevieve developed the fabric on this book's cover from fan-tail shapes, cut

'i don't see myself as an artist — my work sits between craft and design. One of the most defining factors is that more often than not, I look at things as potential end products.'

Genevieve, a Wellington designer—maker and lecturer in textile design, says that compared

Craft Terrorist, *created in response to embroidered denim letters from artist Gabby O'Connor, includes many of the items now banned from airline cabins.*

out of vintage wallpaper then machine-stitched and digitally manipulated with 'an awful lot of masking' into a seamless repeating tile. Without the hand-intervention, she says, digital fabric often feels rather soulless. 'Digital prints can, by nature of the process, be incredibly flat; they need the human touch.'

'Digital prints can, by nature of the process, be incredibly flat; they need the human touch.'

Needless to say, a high degree of competence with the computer is called for — there are several computers in the Aro Valley studio she shares with her partner, a graphic designer and computer graphics artist. One of a pair of former stables in the historically working-class suburb, the huge space allows her to hoard op-shop finds in an assortment of old cabinets, and work at two large tables she made with her impressive collection of power tools, under the direction of her dad. A friend's old, commercial sewing machine stitches the heavy stuff, and one of her current distractions is a donated knitting machine she is teaching herself to use.

Everything Genevieve does is heavily textile-based — even when designing for other media such as the web, she's thinking about pattern, texture, repeats. She often uses both hand and digital processes when exploring themes, materials and processes. She will try out just about anything traditional if it has a potential contemporary application.

Although she was born in Wellington, Genevieve moved with her family to Hawke's Bay at an early age and returned to the capital just before starting college. Shooting off overseas immediately after leaving Hutt Valley High School — where she failed design in the sixth form, 'no textiles or even fashion on offer, only industrial' — gave her not only life experience, but the chance to look at a lot of art, and time to think about what she really wanted to do. By the time she started her degree in her mid-twenties she was deeply committed to textiles, and ended up several years later with First Class Honours and a Massey Scholarship.

Her graduating exhibition took her in a new direction — researching the 'bogan' theme, she discovered how deeply such designs as the state house, a last-minute inclusion, resonated with people. Some of these textiles were brought out for an exhibition at The Dowse marking the 75th anniversary of Hutt Valley High School, including hand screenprinted black T-shirts with 'hutt valley' in Gothic script, a pitbull terrier and a swappa crate. By far, the most popular and enduring image was that of the state house, which is now on Housing New Zealand's stationery list. It was also the central image on billboards for a 2006 exhibition on state houses at the Petone Settlers Museum.

Drawing from her childhood for her Masters degree, Genevieve is exploring how things that have personal relevance can be used to craft contemporary designs that resonate with other people.

Continuing to respond to the craft theme, Genevieve was one of eleven artist friends to whom Gabby O'Connor sent crafted 'touristic artefacts' while travelling overseas in 2004, resulting in an exhibition at City Gallery Wellington's Michael Hirschfeld Gallery. *Craft Terrorist*, now in The Dowse collection, along with a range of her T-shirts, was Genevieve's response to those words and illustrations, stitched in denim, that she received from Gabby. Genevieve chose to use white and dusky pink leather to make a skull and scissors 'gang patch' on a black leather vest, adding a bandolier of craft accoutrements

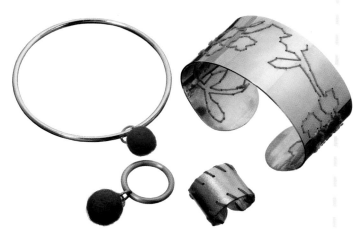

Silver bracelets and rings with detachable felt balls and join-the-dots stitching.

in the utility belt such as knitting and crochet needles, a craft knife, yarn, thread, buttons, needles and multi-tool. A balaclava headpiece has blanket-stitch eye and mouth holes.

Jewellery has become a somewhat self-indulgent passion, though Genevieve is slowly setting herself up with equipment, often crafting work with a textile component — felt bobbles, thread stitching and other unexpected and sometimes found objects. She likes to work on a very small scale, which means using pliers rather than her fingers — a slightly 'hands-off' situation for a hands-on designer.

Genevieve is intrigued at how the act of elevating often overlooked everyday and mundane items, by a shift in materials or scale, changes the way we view them. She currently prefers rings to brooches ('too easy') and works mostly in silver, though a request in 2006 to make her brother's wedding ring gave her the chance to use white gold. ■

Robyn Parker

TWENTY-SEVEN YEARS AFTER ROBYN PARKER WAS FIRST CAPTIVATED BY THE ACT OF CROSSING WEFT YARN ACROSS WARP THREADS, SHE STILL CAN'T GO FOR LONG WITHOUT 'LOOM TIME'.

While others have gone hi-tech, Robyn remains committed to the time-honoured, traditional method of foot-powered handweaving, a skill that saw her making cloth for use in the *Lord of the Rings* movies in 1999.

On her trusty old eight-shaft dobby loom, commissioned in 1984 from Hamilton cabinetmaker Jim Mecchia, Robyn makes the handspun and dyed throws which are her bread and butter line. But she enjoys playing with different techniques and materials for exhibitions, using stainless steel, copper wire and other fibres with wool.

Her latest investment is a beautifully crafted Swedish Oxaback draw loom. There is nothing like it available here — Robyn chose it at the maker's workshop in early 2004 'using a lot of sign language' and it arrived later the same year. She is still experimenting with it, enjoying the facility to create subtle gradations of colour in her fine linen work.

Robyn believes the Swedes are the only weavers still using the draw loom, which has a set of heddles at the back — drawn to create a brocade or damask pattern — as well as the front. 'The Chinese used little boys to stand on top and operate them,' she says. 'They must have been so fast to co-ordinate with the weaver at the front! That was in the days before Monsieur Jacquard automated them.'

Previously a radiographer and qualified pre-school worker, Robyn has been weaving 'pretty much full time' since her youngest child started school in 1983. When her work was well received in exhibitions, she started marketing it through galleries; now most of her pieces are commissioned.

Robyn's first encounter with weaving came during childhood. Her mother reckons she introduced her to it when she was four, but her own earliest memory is as an eight-year-old at school in Hunua. 'I remember the rigid heddle looms we used to make a woollen scarf, and

Work as diverse as this linen cushion, and mercerised cotton Pearl Harbour Explosions 1941 *(overleaf) are woven on a Swedish double harness loom.*

sneaking in at lunchtime to weave.'

She picked up the shuttle in earnest in 1978 when she moved, with her husband David and their children, from Auckland to Plimmerton. Someone was weaving at a new loom when Robyn went along to a local craft group, and she was hooked. 'It was just after my third child was born, because I remember my husband bringing the baby to me so I could feed him during class.'

She started dyeing her own handspun wool to make throws, and painted warps with her Plimmerton friends — including Anna Prussing, whose 'fantastic sense of colour' got the group going. In the struggle to increase skills and professional standards, and to push the boundaries, Robyn has been involved in the formation of local and national guilds — the Port Nicholson Handweavers, followed by the Professional Weavers Network of New Zealand, which she convened for three years.

A teacher of beginners and advanced students at Newlands College night classes, Robyn has also filled in at Massey University's textile design department. She won the Wool Board's Award for Fashion in Wool in 1990 and the same year travelled to Convergence, an American gathering of textile artists in San Jose, on a Queen Elizabeth II Arts Council travel grant. She is also a member of the international Damask Weavers' Network.

Robyn continues to work with Stansborough Fibres, a small family-run company, developing

Pearl Harbour
Explosions 1941.

a range of products using the silky, blue-grey fibres produced by their breed of Gotland sheep, and alpaca fibre. The cloth she designed for them — woven from commercially spun yarn on 1929 Hattersley looms — is used for garments, upholstery, bedcovers, scarves and throws, as well as the *Lord of the Rings'* magic capes.

Sourcing yarns for her own work is an ongoing problem, Robyn says, though the internet has helped enormously. Yarn ordered from Sweden over a year ago has still not arrived; email orders from the United States can come within a week. Coloured linens and cottons can be hard to locate, and she often overdyes existing stock.

One of those artists who would weave even if

she never sold a piece of work, Robyn, who now lives in Whitby, just north of Wellington, is very conscious of the ergonomics of weaving every day. She makes sure she keeps herself 'gymmed and golfed' in order to avoid the fate of friends who have had — literally — back-breaking ends to their weaving careers.

'Weaving for me is a passion, and lifting the profile of handweaving is very important to me. I like to help set up exhibitions and speak to groups such as Rotary and students. I get a lot of pleasure out of sharing my skills and expertise, and often teach small groups for nothing. 'You can get totally obsessed with this thing!' ■

Diana Parkes

DIANA PARKES DYED HER FIRST FABRIC OVER 30 YEARS AGO. IN THOSE DAYS IT WAS JUST A MEANS TO AN END — THESE DAYS IT'S AN END IN ITSELF.

When a particular fabric for an embroidery project was no longer available, it dawned on the Hutt artist that dyeing her own would mean having a constant source. She began doing percentage dyeing — graduated shades of one or two colours — when American quilter Caryl Bryer Fallert came to teach at Quilt Symposium 1993 in Wellington. A range of variegated threads for embroiderers came next.

These days Diana has completely foresworn stitchery in favour of colouring fabric. After convening the Association of New Zealand Embroiderers' Guilds' 2002 biennial conference in Wellington — a four-year undertaking — Diana took stock of her career. She had paid her dues as voluntary editor for four years of *Threads*, the association's magazine. She had already given up regular teaching at night classes and, finding that she was helping other people but not doing any work of her own, she decided to give up embroidery too.

No more heavily stitched, commissioned works like the flags and ceremonial banners she has made since 1981. While she still goes to Guild meetings — she is a life member of the Wellington Embroiderers' Guild — she doesn't want to do embroidery herself any more. 'I felt I had done my dash in that direction.'

Instead, she would set out on an exploration of dyeing through research and practical experimentation. 'Dyeing is a huge field,' Diana says. 'I was beginning to pick up from my reading of overseas magazines how much there was to learn. I like learning — I'm a constant learner.' She decided the ultimate challenge was a three-metre length. 'It's easy enough to do small pieces but something that works over that length is much more difficult.'

The trouble was that people who loved her fabric were afraid to cut into it. So Diana started designing simple garments that made the most of the one-off lengths; her sister, Rosalie Todd, drafted the patterns and made them up in Christchurch. A friend has since joined the enterprise and now Diana also sews up garments. 'It's high priority for me — it's still bread and butter but it's very creative.'

In the last few years, overseas workshops in surface design and shibori have added to Diana's skills — and made her aware of the paucity of discharge processes available here. One dyeing technique is manipulating and securing fabric with stitching before dyeing, using needle and thread, her embroidery heritage. Because she works on a one-off basis, she can accept the 'bit of a gamble' that's involved. 'Dyeing is not an exact science!'

Return of the Queen,
*a collar made of silt sock — an
extremely laborious process
but fit for a Tolkien heroine.*

As well as her exhibition garments, Diana sets herself quite different challenges. The apron in the touring exhibition 'Handycrafts', which was made of paper sugar bags is one of a series she is currently working on.

'I like challenging things that don't really fit into the category of embroidery,' she says; 'unusual materials and unusual concepts that challenge the way you think about that product'. *Return of the Queen* (above), created for an exhibition of collars in 2004, is made of a non-embroidery textile called silt sock, which is used to filter silt in drainage pipes. When landscaping work on her property was being carried out,

she was asked to buy some; ever curious where textiles are concerned, she put a match to a cut end to check the fibre — definitely synthetic. The piece sat around for a while, and as she looked at it she saw its potential as a fringe. Making the collar, beginning with dyeing the silt sock, was an extremely laborious process, but the result is well worth it; fitting indeed for a Tolkien heroine.

The relationship between the idea, the technique and the material is what is important. In the process Diana discovers new ways of working, and different outcomes. Challenging her own and others' preconceptions, with conflicting elements and ideas, is an ongoing motivation. ■

Whorl, *an interpretation of Napier's Norfolk pines.*

Clare Plug

FOR SOME YEARS NOW, CLARE PLUG HAS MADE QUILTS ENTIRELY FROM BLACK FABRIC, WITH LIGHTER AREAS BLEACHED OUT. ONE MIGHT ALMOST WONDER WHETHER SHE IS DEPRESSED. BUT SHE SAYS SHE HAS FAR TOO MANY IDEAS TO EXPLORE TO MOVE OUT OF HER DARK SHADOW-PLAY JUST YET! 'AND OF COURSE,' SHE ADDS, 'BLACK IS A COLOUR USED WIDELY AND TO GREAT EFFECT IN CONTEMPORARY NEW ZEALAND ART.'

Clare's quilts are among the more minimalist of any New Zealand textile artist, yet those who live with them say they never tire of them. The discharge-dyed, whole-cloth quilts — to identify them technically — can evoke intense emotions; they hint at things familiar to many New Zealanders, yet have a universal quality. Their tantalising optical illusions have seen more than one scoop prizes in major American art quilt exhibitions.

Clare's upbringing in Napier, her years of academic study (BScHons in Zoology), her secondary teacher training, and her return to Hawke's Bay after some time overseas — including a summer working in the Shetland and Orkney Islands, where she met her Dutch husband Arie, also an artist — have all contributed to her art. Sometimes the connection is easily seen, as in the quilts that use objects such as the strappy fronds of the Norfolk pines that line the art deco city's Marine Parade, but often it is more tenuous.

The dyeing process, which begins the physical business of quiltmaking, is carried out on the back lawn of the couple's small suburban Napier house, mostly in summer. Clare says it's a rather messy, nerve-wracking and hazardous-to-health business. Even out in the air, she must use old clothes and a respirator to protect herself from fumes and spray. 'There are all sorts of chemicals you can use, but I'm working in the simplest possible way, with household bleach and neutralising chemicals.'

To RH, *one of a series*
honouring New Zealand
artist Ralph Hotere and his
use of black.

Clare Plug on the beach at Napier, the inspiration for many of her quilts.

She may start with ideas from the scrapbooks she keeps — distilled from sketches, her photos and pictures cut from magazines — but once the fabric reveals itself, it tends to dictate the process. She usually makes three or four pieces a day for about a week or two, until she has run out of steam — 'or a deadline is looming!' After that, she auditions them in her lounge and hallway to assess her results and decide whether extra piecing needs to be inserted or if the cloth stands alone. She says there are times when she has to wait a day or two because she is too nervous to cut into them straight away. Clare does her sewing — mostly machine quilting, following a challenge

to try it by visiting tutor Malcolm Harrison while she was at the Eastern Institute of Technology studying craft design — in a small bedroom off the hallway, and dreams of building a studio on the back of the garage.

While the discharge method is fun, it's not very controllable, she says. 'But there's also a wild card thing that can happen, by mistake or inexplicably, and I can push that. It's not a "happy accident", but a gift — you see it and use it.'

Working with whole cloth certainly beats fiddly piecing. 'I'm able to produce more work and faster, running with ideas while they are fresh and hot, and before the personal critic in

Beachfront-inspired
Resonance 5.

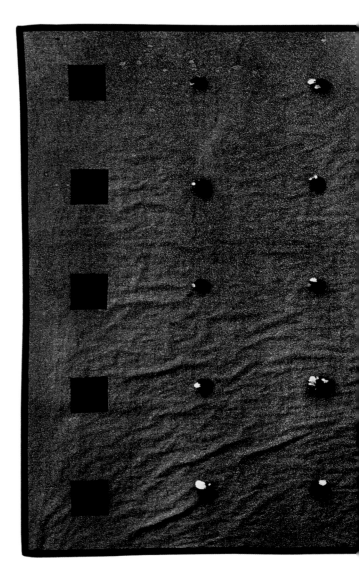

my head gets a chance to discourage me.'

Clare's quilts have the impact of black-and-white photographs, which she has always loved for their 'haunting, timeless quality'. After all, she is working with liquid light. 'Things came right when I took colour out of the mix,' she says. She often works in series, with variations on a theme — such as *Resonance* (five so far), inspired by the Napier beachfront, and *To RH*, a tribute to Ralph Hotere's mastery of illusion and use of the colour 'black' (three so far).

When she began immersing herself in quiltmaking full-time in the nineties, Clare's non-traditional quilts were not well received by her New Zealand peers. The breakthrough came when she saw a catalogue from the 'New Quilt' exhibition at Manly, on Sydney's North Shore. She continues to submit work to their sponsored 'New Quilt' exhibitions.

A workshop with Nancy Crow at the national symposium, in Dunedin in 1991, was the beginning of a continuing connection with the doyenne of American quilting. Clare saved up for two years to get to the two-week Quilt Surface Design Symposium (QSDS) in Ohio, run by Crow and colleague Linda Fowler, and she has been six times since, once with assistance from Creative New Zealand and the rest on work-study grants offered by QSDS.

Mostly, Clare now works towards having solo shows, such as the one at Pakuranga's te tuhi in 2005. As one of this year's Antarctica New Zealand Arts Fellows, Clare — born the day Hillary conquered Everest and given Hilary as her middle name — will travel to the Ice for two weeks in October. In spite of disliking the cold, she is inspired by the frozen continent and expects it to provoke exciting work on her theme, Layers of Protection. ■

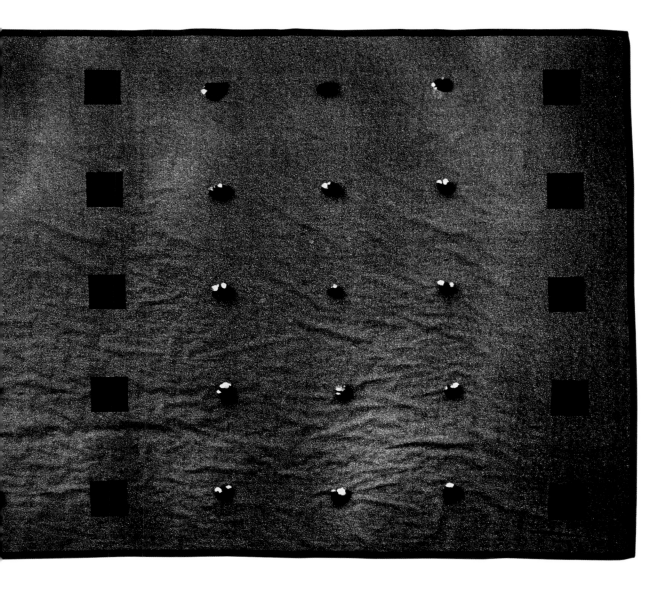

I'm able to produce more work and faster, running with ideas while they are fresh and hot, and before the personal critic in my head gets a chance to discourage me.'

RIGHT: *Gallipoli* honours *Prussing's grandfather Alfred Troughton.*

Anna Prussing

ANNA PRUSSING IS A QUILTMAKER;
SHE DEFINES HERSELF THUS
ON THE ELECTORAL ROLL. FOR
ALTHOUGH THIS PORIRUA WOMAN
STILL MANAGES A MEDICAL
PRACTICE — HER PREVIOUSLY
LISTED OCCUPATION — FOR HER
GP PARTNER, LARRY JORDAN, SHE
NOW CONSIDERS MAKING QUILTS
HER MOST IMPORTANT ROLE. THAT
DOESN'T MEAN SHE NEGLECTS OTHER
PASSIONS. SHE AND LARRY SHARE A
LOVE OF HOUSE AND GARDEN WHICH
INVARIABLY SEES THEM CHOOSING TO
STAY HOME WHEN FRIENDS TAKE OFF
FOR THEIR HOLIDAYS — THEY PREFER
TO PAINT, PLANT, READ AND SIMPLY
ENJOY EACH OTHER'S COMPANY.

 lthough she was a professional weaver for fifteen years, until a back injury and the onset of arthritis put paid to that career, Anna's memory-layered quilts are seldom for sale. Known for combining as many different fabrics in one quilt as she possibly can, she has over the past decade made customised twenty-first birthday quilts for ten nieces and nephews, as well as one for her own son Matthias — there are three more to go. An exhibition of the distinctive quilts, each with a strong focus on the personality and life story of the recipient, is scheduled for Pataka, Porirua, in 2007.

After some years of travelling the country teaching, with all the stitching preparation that involves, Anna now devotes herself to more personal quilts. Her first two have garnered awards: *Mended to Glory* (page 175), in honour of her grandmother, was a finalist in the first Pataka National Award for Excellence in Quilting exhibition and *Gallipoli* (opposite), a memorial to her beloved grandfather, Alfred Troughton, took three awards, including Best of Show, at last year's biennial national quilt symposium

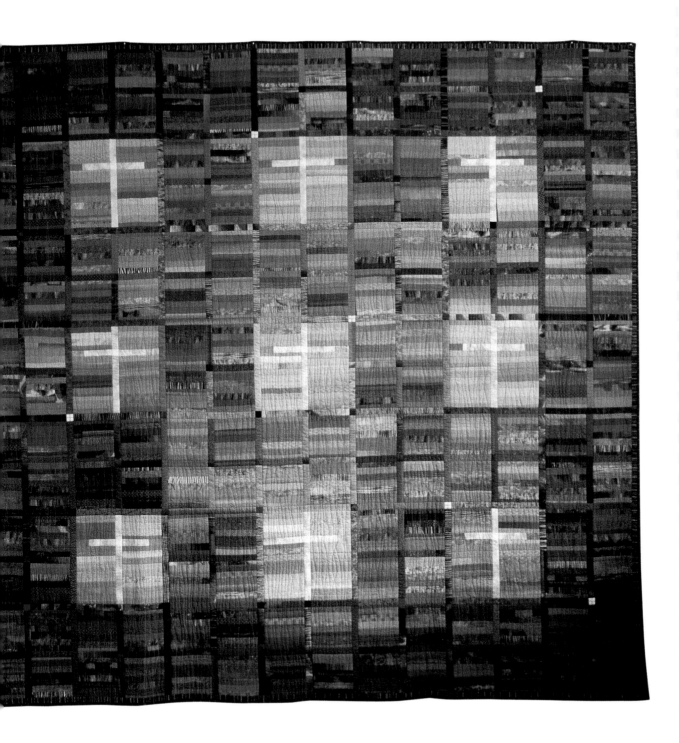

exhibition in Auckland.

Gallipoli's nine white crosses on a stripped background of sludgy greys, dull blues and muddy greens, with the occasional blood-red flash, sombrely evokes the Turkish theatre of war where New Zealand's national identity was forged. Carefully controlled fabric choices are laid out in finely stripped rows of simple blocks suggesting rugged beaches and cliffs — *Gallipoli* also won the Auckland award for Best Use of Colour, an acknowledgement of subtlety rather than brilliance. In addition, the quilt won the award for Best Back Art, with a reverse that incorporates Anna's tribute to the man '. . . who survived Gallipoli, was wounded in France and returned to enrich the life of our family and remind us that ordinary people can do extraordinary things'.

'That was the grimmest winter I ever spent, making that quilt,' Anna says. 'I had it up on the wall in my studio, adding grey on grey. It was raining and I was really sad, missing my grandfather from so long ago. He never really recovered from the war — he was gassed on the Somme and his best friend got blown up on the beach . . .'

The price for such emotional involvement is too high to work at that intensity all the time. Her next personal project, a quilt commemorating her mother — a Cockney war bride who spent nine years in Porirua Hospital — will be especially difficult to make, 'But it has to come out,' she says. The traditional grid pattern Anna uses to

Little Black Hussies,
based on the classic Mammy block, was made for a niece's twenty-first birthday.

tether the personal quilts will lend itself well to such a subject. Making joyful quilts for the new babies — three so far on her side of the family — is a welcome antidote.

Anna's love of textiles goes back to her early childhood, growing up in Wellington. She spent a lot of time with her paternal grandmother, whose German maiden name she later took as her own. As far back as she can remember, Anna was allowed to cut up her grandmother's scraps of silk, velvet, locknit and cotton plisse.

'My grandmother was a milliner and dressmaker. She had a beautiful wardrobe made out of material like silk jersey, wool barathea and gorgeous tweeds, fabrics you don't hear of now. She even had a cedar glove-box, with suede and kid and satin gloves in it. There was a drawer of trimmings for hats — ribbons, veiling, feathers — and she let us use them. She was very generous. My great-aunt who lived with her had her own style, with silk blouses done up with a brooch at the neck. As a treat, I was allowed to iron them.'

Anna started sewing when she was three, with a 'huge' needle. By the time she was five she was allowed to help make her own dresses, using her grandmother's treadle sewing machine with big blocks on it for her feet, and by ten she was sewing all her own clothes, which in those days involved complicated details like facings, darts and buttons. She put herself through university by creating elaborate wedding dresses encrusted

Colour-coded fabrics cover a wall in Anna's Porirua studio.

with embroidery, the fabric purchased from Wellington's late-lamented Thomsons silk shop, 'where you could always go and stroke the Liberty fabrics'.

Like her grandmother, 'a very orderly hoarder, a tidy magpie', Anna refolds all her fabric into neat colour-coded piles before putting it away. There's a particular pleasure in using old clothing, bought from opportunity shops in her neighbourhood, washed, cut up and ironed. 'I don't like it all crumply, it's disrespectful,' she says. 'It has to be cut up, really worn bits cut off, buttons and things saved, then folded as if it came new from the shop.'

For this quilter, fabric has resonances, reminders of place. 'A cushion can remind you

of the bach, polished cotton the excitement and anticipation of a first dance. Cut velvet and patchouli-impregnated Indian muslin invariably transport me back to my hippy days when I lived on Great Barrier Island.

'It's a magic carpet, it can take you back 30 years. For some people it's music — for me it's material.' ■

RIGHT: **Mended to Glory** *recalls Anna Prussing's grandmother, for whom darning was a virtue.*

The Exhibition Opening *was first exhibited in 2004 at 'Yardage' in Wellington.*

Marilyn Rea-Menzies

'ALMOST AN OBSESSION, CERTAINLY A PASSION AND MOST DEFINITELY A WAY OF LIFE,' IS HOW CHRISTCHURCH TAPESTRY WEAVER MARILYN REA-MENZIES DESCRIBES HER AFFAIR WITH TAPESTRY.

n 1994, as she prepared to move to Christchurch to set up New Zealand's only tapestry workshop, Marilyn defined her commitment to tapestry weaving thus. She still feels just as passionate about what she sees as the supreme textile form — especially when it comes to architectural settings.

Tapestry is a form that has been around for millennia, keeping people warm in draughty castles, and decorating large open spaces; fragments have been found dating back as far as 5000 BC, demonstrating a textile of extraordinary durability.

'The content and structure of the work are so interdependent that one cannot exist without the other, and there is something quite satisfying in creating a whole piece from nothing.'

———

'Making is no different now to what it was generations ago and the design possibilities are endless,' Marilyn says. 'The content and structure of the work are so interdependent that one cannot exist without the other, and there is something quite satisfying in creating a whole piece from nothing.'

She says the architectural process of building a tapestry — actually constructing the fabric and image together so that the two are physically and visually inseparable — relates very strongly to the process of constructing and building our lives. Some of Marilyn's largest tapestries foil the hard edges of buildings around New Zealand: *The Baycourt Tapestries* (1983–85) in Tauranga's municipal Baycourt Theatre; *Women of Marlborough* (1995) in the Marlborough District Council, and *The Millennium Tapestry* (1999–2000), designed by Philip Trusttum, which hangs in the mayoral chamber of Christchurch City Council.

It was when this veteran weaver heard in the late eighties that the Aotea Centre was giving its major Robert Ellis-designed tapestry commission to the Melbourne-based Victorian Tapestry Workshop that Marilyn decided it was time to establish such a facility here. She

eventually set up The Christchurch Tapestry Workshop in June 1998, in the South Quad's Chemistry Building in the Arts Centre.

A primary school teacher with a Diploma of Fine Arts Preliminary qualification, Marilyn began to teach drawing, design and weaving at high school night classes, and to guilds around the country, while based in Tauranga in the eighties. After setting up Viewpoint Arts Studio there, she began taking on polytechnic weaving students for work experience. She moved to Picton to join up with the International Weaving School of New Zealand, taking with her Glenora Craft, the handweaving supply agency she had previously set up in partnership with Birgite Armstrong and Kay Ward. Leaving Picton three and a half years later, she moved to Christchurch, finally setting up her workshop/studio where you can still find her at work.

While commissions are usually designed in consultation with the individual or group wanting the work, Marilyn started an ambitious series of collaborations in 1995 with nine artists, most of them Christchurch based, with the intention of introducing them to tapestry as an exciting and viable art form. The artists she

One of a series of collaborations with Canterbury visual artists, The Railway Cup Tapestries *interpret Rudolf Boelee's images.*

worked with included Julia Morison, Rudolf Boelee and Philip Trusttum. The exhibition resulting from these collaborations, 'Primary Connections', was shown at Christchurch's Centre of Contemporary Art (CoCA) in 2004–5. *The Railway Cup Tapestries* (left) brings together Dutch New Zealander Rudolf Boelee's individual images of the fifties icon, from the time when 'everything was possible and life here was good'. *The Exhibition Opening* is Marilyn's own work, first exhibited at the Combined Textiles Exhibition 'Yardage' at the Academy of Fine Arts in Wellington in 2004.

'In today's climate of instant gratification, weaving tapestry is almost an act of rebellion,' Marilyn says. 'However, the balance between the work of the mind, the heart, and the hands, the tactile qualities in the crossing of threads, the optical blending of colours, depth and richness of tonal values and exquisite gradations of colour that are possible with tapestry, all make this medium so exciting and exhilarating to work with.' ∎

Commercially-embroidered houses record a family's residential history.

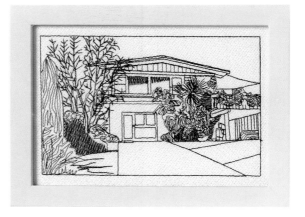

Monique Redmond

AN INTEREST IN WHERE MEMORIES ARE STORED LED MONIQUE REDMOND TO PHOTOGRAPH HOUSES WHERE HER FAMILY HAS LIVED, THEN HAVE THEM CONVERTED TO CLOTH BY A DIGITAL EMBROIDERY PROCESS. HOWEVER, SHE DOESN'T CONSIDER HERSELF FIRST AND FOREMOST A TEXTILE ARTIST.

he houses that we have occupied afford us our memories and remind us of our family's lifetimes,' says Monique, who has been using textile-related methods in her practice for twelve years — embroidery, tapestry work stools, even one quilted piece. But textiles are only the means to an end, and because that end has been for some time an interest in the domestic, stitch inevitably comes into use.

'It's a commentary about the objects as much as a method,' she says. If stitch suits her purpose

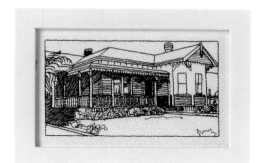
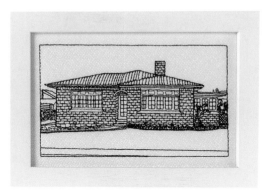

or concept, she uses it; if other methods, such as photography, are better, she employs those.

Housing 2003 (pictured) was exhibited at Auckland Museum in 2005 as one of three exhibitions making up 'The New Zealand House'. The eight black-on-white cotton drill works were embroidered to photographic scale by a firm that makes sports badges, working from photos found in family albums. 'I wanted as much photographic accuracy as possible but with a reduction of detail akin to embroidery,' says Monique. 'I wanted to do it myself but many places were run by people who preferred not to let me near their equipment! The person who did it understood what I was after though.'

The houses were given titles appropriate to family members of the period when each was lived in by Monique's extended family — names such as Ulla, Mary, Ivy, Vi and, inevitably, Monique — along with the street name and suburb, as a reference to place.

Monique usually creates installations in public spaces as well as exhibiting in galleries. Some years ago she lined up jars of preserves in a

work titled *Spectacular Blossom, 1995* — fruit jellies, made by co-operative friends and family — with text from Allen Curnow, Katherine Mansfield and Bruce Mason sandblasted onto the jars, one word on each jar, arranged on shelves in the format of the printed text.

Gardening, another domestic activity that unites New Zealanders, also interests Monique, especially the recognition of 'things you don't necessarily notice the first time you see them'. The ubiquitous hydrangea — a 'front yard trophy' that has survived and thrived since the first white settlers brought it to these shores — can be found in gardens from council houses to 'two-storeyed large villas'. When in flower, their presence invites you to look at them; 'They sort of wave out at you,' Monique reckons.

Monique has documented the hydrangea in flower in Auckland, Coromandel and Southland; after photographing 300 hydrangeas from a moving car, she arranged the images into three suburban grids within one large photographic work, titled *Hydrangea Suburb 2006*. In 2005, she installed 90 potted indoor flowering hydrangeas

LEFT: Isabella,
Apihai St in Orakei.

RIGHT: Urban
Typography I

in the Great Hall of the Old Museum Building at Massey University in Wellington, as part of her Massey University Fine Arts residency where she stayed at the Rita Angus Cottage.

As part of her interest in how we occupy landscapes, in 'spaces lost and found', Monique is exploring ideas of how we move around — the periods of transition from one place to another, how we travel familiar routes, the way we navigate — and consequently deliberately photographs places and objects in space, while she drives around various suburban zones.

Urban Topography 2005(above) captures three of those 'embroidered moments' in these handstitched embroideries. Drawn with a series of linear stitches, for their autographic nature, she says the motorways themselves don't have to be embroidered, but that the embroidery itself has the nature of a drawn moment about it. 'It has the ability to draw people in,' she says. 'There's a narrative around stitch. A lot of contemporary artists are using embroidery for its illustrative ability and in other ways — it is the ultimate in autographical mark-making.'

As a Senior Lecturer in Visual Arts to undergraduate and Masters students at Auckland University of Technology, Monique works on her own art in concentrated blocks of time around her teaching schedule, which also includes specialising in sculpture on the Bachelor of Visual Arts course. She has been a teacher at tertiary level in New Zealand since 1992.

Monique had a crafty childhood — both her grandfathers were makers of a kind, and her grandmothers did virtually every handcraft, except tapestry and embroidery. Although she has at times shifted out of stitched work, embroidery keeps figuring somehow. 'They are media I'm interested in, the personalised, autographic nature of it.' ∎

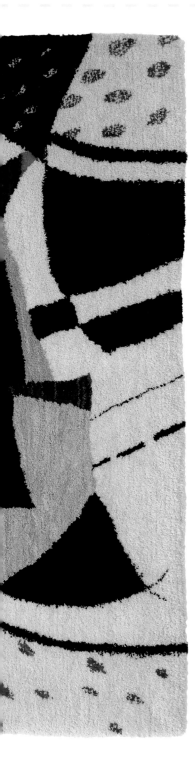

Jocelyn Seccombe

MUSIC AND ART BATTLED FOR DOMINANCE IN JOCELYN SECCOMBE'S LIFE FOR MANY YEARS UNTIL, IN THE END, SHE CAME TO ACCEPT THAT EACH FEEDS THE OTHER.

Ch'ien, *a hand-tufted wool rug.*

When Jocelyn has had enough of her textile work she plays her flute; when it gets too cold to keep tufting a rug in her garage, she comes inside and sits down at her sewing machine, paints or picks up lesson plans for her adult education art classes in drawing, painting and colour.

Having started a fine arts degree before taking up flute study at the age of 20, Jocelyn thinks she will always paint, but she loves the sensual side of textiles. Unfortunately, she says, embroidery ends up behind glass and you have to 'feel it with your eyes'.

Rugs are another matter. Jocelyn first tried the tufting technique at Wellington Polytechnic in 1992, after graduating with a Diploma in Textile Design. Having seen the technical difficulties encountered by the students who chose rugs as part of their graduating topic, Jocelyn waited until she had finished her portfolio before tackling the challenge of handling the power gun. It took her just a

'I do love the look of rugs, they have such a presence in a room,' she says.
'I started with embroidery but then I wanted to work bigger.'

week to tuft her first rug. These days she works much more slowly, with an eggbeater-like hand tool called, ironically, a 'Rumplestiltskin Speedneedle', which allows her to incorporate more detail than the power gun does.

'I do love the look of rugs, they have such a presence in a room,' she says. 'I started with embroidery but then I wanted to work bigger.'

The (much smaller) embroideries Jocelyn currently works on are machine-embroidered on felt she makes herself, from merino slivers. The machine embroidery was also taken up while she was at polytechnic — responding to the challenge to try something new as part of the course requirements, Jocelyn took a class with Laura Hudson back home in Palmerston North one weekend. She loves the freedom of machine embroidery: 'I can make it up as I go along, or plan it in advance; it is akin to drawing, which I love, and also similar to painting, except the colours don't dry up while I go off to earn my living.'

Felt, however, is something Jocelyn has worked in since the seventies when she made — very seventies this — a pair of boots. 'Felt is a wonderful medium — it can be 3D or flat, it's very nice to sew on and it gives a three-dimensional quality to a work, something like quilting.'

A childhood in the country gave Jocelyn the feel and smell for wool, plucked off fences. She took up spinning in her twenties, dyeing with natural dyes then moving to synthetic dyes. She has always painted as well, especially when it comes to designing her embroideries and rugs. Cutting up and rearranging work is a favoured approach — the embroideries *Spring Song* and *Backstage* and the rug *Ch'ien* (page 184) are all the result of this design process.

Jocelyn was invited to contribute work to the 2004 exhibition 'Art Embroidery — A Wide Focus on New Territories' at Alexander Palace, London, which toured the UK and Europe as part of the annual Knitting and Stitching Show. Exhibitions and commissions serve to keep her focussed in the same way as upcoming concerts do for a musician. In many ways it is the visual equivalent of music, 'something that is arresting and holds the attention and that is fresh'.

'The potential of materials is very seductive,' she says. 'But when you get down to it, it calls for a lot of practice and discipline, because all materials have their particular strengths and limitations, and you have to know what they are and work with them.'

Jocelyn says she sees what she does as a tiny part of the ongoing process of creation by mankind and in nature. 'It gives me great pleasure to work with the materials, using colour against colour, creating rhythms, harmonies, discords, resolutions, little surprises, and expressing the kind of delight and energy that make life worth living.' ∎

Sonatina, *machine embroidery on handmade felt.*

The moods of the coastline are interpreted in Ailie Snow's Apparent Horizons *series.*

Ailie Snow

RAGGED, TORN, STAINED, DISCARDED — THE RAW MATERIALS OF AILIE SNOW'S CLOTH AND STITCH WORKS HAVE DEFINITELY SEEN BETTER DAYS.

She has even been known to bury her silk fabric, or to wrap it with rusty nails, and otherwise encourage degradation as part of the process of adding history to her stories in cloth.

'It's really hard to say what I do,' she says. 'I use cloth and stitch to tell a story — in lots of different ways.' How about textile poet? That's what writer Jeanette DeNicolis Meyer calls Ailie, and it sums up the multi-layered, essential nature of her work.

The *Ladies* series (pages 190 and 191), of which she has made around 50 over several years, fitted around other projects, uses ethereal shapes, layered and stitched, of printed and torn scraps that evoke a mood, season, or the faintest whisper of someone else's story, to convey the Lady of the title she chooses. That they are headless matters not at all. And the

word Lady itself — rejected by feminists — is loaded with allusion, from courtly love poetry to Shakespeare, adding to the potential meaning.

Supporting and underpinning this practice are Ailie's visual journals and fabric books, which develop her observational side and feed the more formal stories. She has been compiling these stacks of thick accretions — some incorporating plaster so the pages crackle as they are turned — for the last eight years, an extension of the written journals she has kept as far back as she can remember.

Ailie's classes are in demand around New Zealand and occasionally overseas. Some classes are based on the book arts, some are about creating with cloth and stitch, and some combine both. Working from a home studio that looks out into trees, on the edge of a reserve, Ailie surrounds herself with an organised jumble of resources — fabric scraps from a quilter friend,

LADY CAUGHT IN THE WEB OF WINTER

'I think it's important to love the process. Stitching is quite a meditative process, it allows you to be designing as you go, and be involved while you do it.'

The **Ladies** *series uses printed, torn, layered and stitched shapes to whisper stories* — Lady caught in the web of winter *(above)* and Lady emerging from the woods of winter *(right).*

remnants gifted at workshops, op-shop scarves, fabrics collected over the years, and lots of paper for her notebooks and diaries.

Ailie's 'Apparent Horizons' exhibition at te tuhi in early 2005 incorporated the contents of her quilter friend Louise's rubbish bag — handstitched onto canvas textured with gesso and paint — to communicate the moods and openness of the coastline.

A trained teacher, Ailie taught primary school in New Zealand and overseas before beginning her textile practice. 'I always loved art lessons and decorating the classroom and putting the children's work on the wall,' she says. While she enjoys reading and discussing papers and theses with friends who are involved in fine arts postgraduate studies, Ailie is not interested in more study herself for the moment. 'I'm more humanistic in my approach to my work. Some of that stuff is too far removed from work and life, and I'm into work and life.'

While she is now experienced in many textile forms — knitting, felting, paper and bookbinding among them — Ailie started out as a knitwear designer, knitting her designs by hand rather than machine, and she still stitches by hand only. 'I haven't used a machine in a long time. I'm not a quilter, I was never really happy using a sewing machine. I love the physical act of stitching; needle in, needle out.

'I think it's important to love the process. Stitching is quite a meditative process, it allows you to be designing as you go, and be involved while you do it. The hands are doing it while the mind is creating the next bit — it's a journey.' ■

LADY EMERGING FROM THE WOODS OF WINTER

Sonia Snowden

SONIA SNOWDEN CONSIDERS HER
HIGHEST ACHIEVEMENT TO BE
SUPERVISING THE REPLICATION OF
230 SQUARE METRES OF TUKUTUKU
WEAVING — 76 PANELS — FOR
RANGIATEA CHURCH, IN OTAKI,
AFTER IT ROSE AGAIN FROM THE
ASHES IN THE NEW MILLENNIUM.

nder her guidance and leadership, 130,000 strands of kiekie fibre were used to reconstruct the 150-year-old panels. Most of the 23 weavers required training in the work ethic and also in the etiquette required to comply with tikanga and kawa (protocol). As kaihautu, Sonia thoroughly enjoyed herself, even though she was working every day for six days a week — about 80 hours each week — and the weavers' job was finished in 2002. The church was reopened in 2004. Sonia had previously been in charge of the preparation of the kiekie fibre — an epiphyte that grows in the bush — used to weave the panels. 'It was a big, big job,' she says.

Sonia Snowden, Ngati Whatua and Nga Puhi, has lived in Otaki for 35 years. She was born in Kawakawa and brought up by her tupuna (old folk) at Waikare in the Bay of Islands, coming south gradually through her teens until she got to Otaki. She had seen weaving done

Sonia Snowden's finely woven kete have earned her the right to use the Toi Iho label.

— mats for the marae and piupiu for the school haka group — but was too young to be interested herself. 'You have to come to it when you are ready,' she says.

Sonia was ready by 1978 when she went to Otaki College, as a young mother with a baby, to adult day classes in te reo. Her teacher, the late Hiko Hohepa, got a small group of the language students interested in weaving, then took them each school holidays to Rotorua, to learn by preparing the flax and working on mats on his two home marae, Mataikotare and Ruamata. They were taught there by Emily Schuster, at the New Zealand Arts and Crafts Institute in Whakarewarewa.

'I learnt the art of weaving a whariki there before I ever made a basket,' Sonia says. 'Everybody was making kete then. So I went

Another exquisitely woven kete of kiekie fibre.

to the top first!' The need was so great that beginners were working on the meeting house whariki that are usually the last thing a novice is taught, because there were not enough weavers who could meet the demand for meeting houses under refurbishment. Of the four 'keen ones' chosen by Hiko to go from Otaki — Tungia Baker, Raukura Leather, Horiana Joyce and Sonia — only Sonia is still alive.

Sonia, who is now considered one of the country's best fine weavers, made one of many kete, raffled it for a bus fare to Rotorua for more tutelage in kete weaving. 'I got a blessing to do that fundraising. 'There was no one down here

to tutor us. It took me ages to get it right — I must have made a thousand ketes before I was satisfied.'

For most of the nineties Sonia taught weaving for various trusts in Otaki, then helped teach diploma and degree students at Te Wananga o Raukawa at Te Whare Toi. 'I was there if they needed any help,' she says. She resigned from there to become kaihautu for Rangiatea.

Sonia is currently teaching others, with the assistance of a grant from Te Waka Toi Creative New Zealand, to weave whariki for their marae in the Raukawa rohe around Otaki, three weekends a month. A dozen people on one marae and

'For me harakeke, kiekie and pingao have taken me on a wonderful, exciting journey throughout my years of weaving.'

fourteen on the other work hard to create the special-occasion whariki that will be used for events such as tangihanga. The project will take about eight to nine months.

The oldest weaver, Kuia Morehu, Maud Miratana, is nearly 100 and comes along in her wheelchair. 'We give her a glove and a knife so she can prepare the flax,' Sonia says. The youngest are 16- to 18-year-olds, and some mothers whose whanau look after the children so they can concentrate on their work. Men come to support, but in spite of Sonia's encouragement, won't join in. 'I tell them men were the first to weave,' she chuckles. 'They wove fishing nets. But they don't believe me.'

Sonia is now trying to work out how to protect the mats from carpet, since most meeting house floors are now carpeted, unlike the older wooden ones. 'The carpet doesn't help — it catches and frays something terrible,' she says. 'You've got to be aware of that.'

When it comes to Sonia's own work, she snatches time between other commitments, but there's not enough time to produce work to meet requests for exhibition pieces.

Working in harakeke (flax), pingao (the golden beach grass that grows up the coast) and kiekie, she dyes some of her fibre in a pot using red, yellow and black synthetic dyes.

For the marae work, there is plenty of harakeke growing by the side of the road or in gardens to meet the demand locally. Sonia has a couple of boilers she takes to the marae for preparation, which is done about a week before the work begins.

'You've got to know your weather before you go out to cut,' she says. 'Rainy weather is no good for the drying stage.' The harakeke is cut, sized, tied and boiled then cooled in cold water before being softened with a knife. Then it is hung on the clothesline to dry and bleach to a creamy colour. When thoroughly dried, the prepared flax is put in bags until required.

'For me harakeke, kiekie and pingao have taken me on a wonderful, exciting journey throughout my years of weaving,' Sonia says. 'Many expert weavers have helped me on this journey and filled my kete with the knowledge of weaving. They have bestowed blessings on me that have allowed me to continue with my work. I shall endeavour to do my best to share this knowledge for it is not mine to keep.' ■

He taonga tuku iho
Na nga tupuna
Mo nga uri whakatipu
A treasure handed down
From our ancestors
For the up and coming generations.

Juliet Novena Sorrel

There is something other-worldly about Juliet Novena Sorrel's dolls. When you discover that their creator often dresses up in elaborate costumes and performs on stilts, and that she also makes elegant copper and rusty wire sculptures with human faces, you start to realise why.

J uliet now lives in Seacliff, a small village north of Dunedin overlooking the ocean, with her partner and two children. She has finally built her own studio — two-storeyed at that — next door, and with a potbelly stove to keep her warm she can work through the coldest southern winters. While her children, Florence and Lichen, are at school, Juliet works on the dolls she first started making over fifteen years ago.

Juliet began to sell the ceramic, cloth and stick dolls around six years ago, although they have always been part of the art and sculptural installations that have been her practice since she attended Canterbury School of Fine Art. She dresses papier-mâché bodies, with stick legs, in unembellished muslin and voile — often tea-dyed — because she likes the way those fabrics colour with age.

Some of her dolls have softer bodies, and plaster or ceramic arms and heads, so they can be manipulated. Cut out freehand, each is proportionally different — some body parts are sculpted with gib-stopping compound to create character, and some dolls become marionettes, suspended and ornamental.

Straw and tussock grass become skirts, old dressmaking patterns are used for garments, wool and upholstery stuffing turns into hair — all because they have an existing history. She makes latex moulds to make plaster-cast families of dolls, which then become individuals in her hands. Made in batches of two to ten, these are sometimes exhibited as groups. 'They are like sisters, family groups with a shared history,' she says. 'The use of old lace, tea stain and cloth remnants refers to the history of domestic arts, domestic labour and mothering.' They are not pretty — they are earthy and real.

Juliet believes her creations appeal because

they are not perfect: 'They are individual and handmade.' And poignant and mysterious, looking like they might have been buried in the bottom of the toybox or lost in the garden.

The fairy story mythology of dolls is as much part of Juliet's performance art as her visual and installation work. Juliet has a history of incorporating dolls as figures into larger sculptures. Earth boats carry a family of cloth-bodied figures, stick houses enclose ceramic or stick figures. In performances, dolls encased in lighted glass boxes are unearthed, dolls emerge from giant piles of sticks, or are revealed from the inner folds of costumes.

'The dolls symbolise relationships between people, families, and the land. My use of found or time-worn materials evokes a sense of history, the insignificance of humanity in contrast with the power of nature and the passage of time.' ■

Juliet Novena Sorrel's dolls can be poignant and mysterious, or disconcertingly like us.

Sue Spigel

Where do you start when endeavouring to capture the history of a building or a place in cloth? To mark the anniversaries of her cathedral and her adopted city, American-born Sue Spigel began by reading Michael King's *penguin history of new zealand*. Then she went back to a history of the universe.

from there came the ideas that inspired the eight 'compositions' exhibited in Christchurch's cathedral from March to Easter 2006. From *In The Beginning*, through *Migrations* to *A Journeying Cloak for Gaia and the Archangel Gabriel*, the impetus came from Sue's desire to honour the part city and cathedral play in the lives of their communities, on the occasion of their 150th and 125th anniversaries respectively.

The award-winning quilter, born and raised in Michigan but resident in Christchurch since 1978, had been working with Russian artist Galina Kim on occasional exhibitions over the last three years since she fell in love with Galina's art at an exhibition and bought one of her paintings. *Merging Traditions* — which took a year

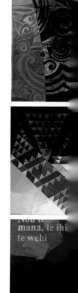

Merging Traditions is a series of eight painted, printed and stitched panels depicting subjects such as Migrations *(top, left),* Tangata Whenua *(bottom left),* Arrival of the English *(right).*

Sue used to make half a dozen quilts a year for exhibitions and contests — as much for the business as anything, she says. Now she does not print cloth for sale, doesn't teach ('I do what I feel like and teaching is not what I feel like') and will not enter quilts in an exhibition if there is any competitive element involved. 'Now they are mainly made for myself and to express myself,' she says. 'I don't care if anybody else likes them or not.'

Now living in Governors Bay on Banks Peninsula, Sue enjoys working in her garden, growing veggies and getting her hands dirty. 'And I love compost,' she says, pronouncing it the American way to rhyme with post. 'It's death and life all at once, the whole process of transformation and new life.'

Sue works on big processes — dyeing and screenprinting — in her home studio, saving stamping, block printing, making one-off garments and smaller quilts, for her studio in the city's Arts Centre. The exception to Sue's new way of working was the altar cloth, commissioned for Christchurch Cathedral, which she completed recently — a very large three- by five-metre panel.

She makes more quilts now, working in panels which are easier to handle, 'dream-like snippets of illumination', using words and sometimes a bit of poetry, or biblical quotations. 'The idea behind that is that we never see the whole thing that's going on. It's about life and how I see it, about life and the earth and the self.' ■

to plan and four months to make — is the fifth project to combine Galina's paintings and Sue's printed and stitched fabric panels.

In setting out to tell the story of the cathedral — 'both good and bad; it was not all nice and pretty' — Sue read widely before starting: King's *Penguin History of New Zealand*, a mathematical cosmologist's history of the universe, medieval scholar Meister Eckhart, Teilhard de Chardin, Jung, the Hebrew Prayer Book. She says quilts can include 'a lot of ugliness', depending on how you read them, whereas not too many works using words can do that without causing offence.

A stitcher since the age of four, when she started making dolls' clothes on her mother's machine, Sue was a practising speech therapist with a Masters degree when she came to New Zealand in the seventies. She taught herself quilting, mostly from books, in the late eighties.

Yanny Split

YANNY SPLIT MAY WELL BE THE MOST ACCEPTED WORLD OF WEARABLE ARTS
ENTRANT IN THE AWARDS' HISTORY. SINCE FIRST ENTERING IN 1991, THE
HUNTLY ARTIST HAS HAD OVER 33 GARMENTS ACCEPTED — SIX IN 1995 —
AND IN 1993 SHE WON THE WOOL SECTION.

With a string of other fashion awards under her handcrafted belt, Yanny regularly teaches, organises an annual nine-day summer school that has helped put the Waikato town of Raglan on the map and set up an arts trail — launched in 2005 by Prime Minister Helen Clark — to raise the profile of local artists and bring visitors into her adopted town.

She won a national Business and Professional Women's award for setting up the Huntly Switched On To Artz awards. She is adult community education co-ordinator for Huntly College (where she tutors the quilters and patchworkers group), chair of the Creative Communities assessment committee for the Waikato, and a trustee for Arts Waikato. In 2007, she will again bring the focus on Huntly, when she moves her summer school there from Raglan.

Yanny stands out for her personal style — tall, with her greying blonde hair tied up with one of her silk scarves, and colourful clothes to match. 'I love colour and making my own fabric using dyes and surface design. I keep experimenting just to increase the possibilities in my own design.'

Yanny has played with every kind of textile technique you can name — felting, weaving, knitting, crochet and embroidery. She dyes and manipulates yarns and experiments with almost anything to get just the look she wants — a bag of drinking straws becomes a wearable arts entry; laminated, freeze-dried fruit and vegetables are about to be incorporated into one of her *Seven Jackets of the Week*, each made using a different technique.

Shown here are *Tuesday* and *Friday* jackets plus a bag in the technique she will use for *Monday's jacket*. Tuesday is daisy day, with over 200 flowers ('Much more than I expected when I counted up!') worked over a sixties daisy wheel — a bit like a French knitting ring — found at a garage sale. The daisies are worked of torn-up, hand-dyed silk, then mounted on a jacket of green raw silk on tulle. The shawl collar and cuffs are shibori dyed on a pole — just one of the ways of making the pleated fabric — then redyed. Yanny says she likes to leave the pleats in rather than pressing the fabric flat.

Friday's jacket is of a hand-dyed raw silk known as 'throwster's waste' — offcuts not normally used, which Yanny likes for its texture — and mulberry silk. Coloured silk is manipulated to look 'like little gardens'. The bottom and cuffs are of stiffened silk paper. A watering can button completes the theme.

Yanny's 1994 wedding to her Kiwi sweetheart Alan Coates, an antiques and collectables dealer she met at a nightclub — she was bored and he decided she needed cheering up — was a full-scale, wearable art affair. The 250 guests — many of them artists, plus one of Yanny's eleven siblings from Holland — came in garments gorgeous, outrageous, vibrant and sometimes plain crazy for an outdoor wedding at Basque Park in Newton, Auckland.

Since 1996, the pair have lived and worked together at home in the small town of Huntly, where they moved, for financial reasons, from a large Auckland warehouse. There's still enough space to accommodate both their passions — the back is basically Alan's business space, full of the collections he sells at weekend antique and collectable fairs, while Yanny has the sunnier double room in front as her studio.

Born in the Netherlands in 1947, Yanny originally trained as a window dresser, display painter and flower arranger before studying at art school in Rotterdam under one of the country's top fashion designers, Cargelli. She organised the first fashion show ever held in a Dutch art gallery.

In 1987, Yanny came to New Zealand and settled in Auckland, working in a boutique in partnership with her friend Doris de Pont. 'After a month I knew I was not a commercial designer — I am not a dressmaker. The business of running a shop was not for me.'

Going solo, however, took a little longer. Her friend Susan Holmes suggested she might get her name in the public eye by entering Nelson's Wearable Arts show. 'I did it straightaway — and I was hooked!'

Similarly with the Benson and Hedges awards — later the Smokefree Fashion awards — thirteen successful appearances and a Wool Section winner in 1990 with a stunning cream ensemble. The list goes on — New Zealand and Australian wool awards, Mohair awards, Fibre and Fleece, Pasifika, Trash to Fashion and

Norsewear, becoming more avant-garde each time.

Made as a statement rather than for everyday wear, Yanny's clothing is bought by overseas buyers, yet she would keep doing it even if there was no outlet. She believes entering awards is important for all artists — 'Getting your name in a catalogue helps raise your profile' — and has a healthy attitude to rejection: 'Enter as much as possible and get over it if you're not accepted.'

Having set herself the challenge of making 'a jacket for each day of the week', Yanny is planning to make a dozen outfits for her family that reflect the diverse characters of her brothers and sisters. She hopes that by asking them to answer ten questions about themselves she will be able to create garments that are as recognisable as the individuals that inspired them. ■

LEFT: *Much more than a daisy a day for Yanny Split's* Tuesday jacket.

Friday's jacket *uses mulberry silk and throwster's waste — raw silk offcuts — and silk paper.*

One of Suzanne Tamaki's fiery feather and shell neckpieces, sold under the Toi Iho label.

Suzanne Tamaki

THE YEAR 2006 SAW SUZANNE TAMAKI REALISE HER DREAM OF TAKING PASIFIKA FASHION TO THE WORLD, WHEN SHE TRAVELLED WITH FIVE OTHER ARTISTS TO THE OPENING OF AN EXHIBITION OF 21ST-CENTURY MAORI AND PACIFIC ART AND CULTURE — AT THE VERY HEART OF BRITISH ACADEMIA.

oogle her name and you get a deluge of links. The list of creative arts Suzanne Tamaki (Maniapoto, Tuhoe, Te Arawa) has explored just keeps growing — fashion, costume design, solo exhibitions, teaching wearable art and indigenous design, choreographing dance, creating jewellery.

Suzanne has exhibited consistently at The Dowse since 1997, has won the Westfield Style Pasifika fashion award (2003) and Fashion in the Field at her local Otaki Maori Racing Club meeting (2006), and taken workshops with indigenous peoples in Colombia, South America.

But Pasifika Styles 2006 — a festival that will actually extend over two years — is her most ambitious project yet. In April 2006, a life-sized wharenui of carved perspex was created by George Nuku to connect the Cambridge

University Museum of Archaeology and Anthropology's unparalleled Oceanic collections with New Zealand's best contemporary artists and craftspeople.

Suzanne never intended to get into the fashion field — she says she was simply making a political statement when she used checked blankets, men's top hats and pheasant feathers in her earliest garments. A series of five of these is

now in Te Papa's collection.

'People respond really well to blankets,' she says. 'They keep evolving — always blanket stitch, sometimes pompoms like pois.' A new piece, made for Cambridge, is called *Bicultural Rap Remix*.

The Otaki artist, and mother of three, has become synonymous with the creation and promotion of indigenous style. She often recycles Made-in-New-Zealand elements, such

'From the catwalk in Otaki to the footpaths of Paris, a train across Italy to Wellington railway station — who knows where your passions will take you?' Suzanne says. 'As long as you remember where you come from.'

as men's wool suits adorned with ceremonial buttons — all with New Zealand associations — in the shape of Aotearoa, making a statement that is both political and fashionable.

In 2002, as part of the Magdalena Pacifica Women's International Festival in Colombia, Suzanne ran cross-cultural workshops in creating body adornment and wearable art using material from the local environment. 'Except they were all living in the city and there was no plant material so we used a lot of plastic. We wrote a performance based on earth, water, air and fire — it lasted about half an hour and we performed it in a stadium to thousands. It was awesome.'

Jewellery is Suzanne's latest adornment obsession, using feathers, shells and teeth to make exotic headpieces, neckpieces, cuffs and sensual bikinis. The glowing neckpiece of red feathers with shells (page 205) was featured in a Toi Iho brand showcase in Te Papa in 2006. Suzanne's latest commission was a request from the British Museum to create work in response to the oldest known existing Maori manu aute (kite), from Te Arawa, which is in the museum's collection. This work is a 2-metre x 2-metre piece entitled *Wahine Manu — Bird Woman*.

For last year's Pacific Arts Festival in Belau,

Micronesia, Suzanne — representing Aotearoa as one of eight 'most exciting emerging visual artists' and co-ordinator of the New Zealand contribution to the Pacific Fashion Show — created a G-string with feathers and teeth, a reference to Hinenuitepo, the Maori goddess of death.

On the other hand, she's equally likely to whip together a necklace from such common materials as bottletops off Tui beer, a feat that featured in *Maiden Mangatainoka* the Oceania category at this year's Cleveland Art Awards in Dunedin. She had friends saving up the red caps so she could take spares to Cambridge to give as gifts.

Where to from here? 'From the catwalk in Otaki to the footpaths of Paris, a train across Italy to Wellington railway station — who knows where your passions will take you?' Suzanne says. 'As long as you remember where you come from.' ∎

Greg Semu's photograph of Kahui Itirawa Tahau–Blackler (Tuwharetoa and Ngai Tuhoe) for
'Aotearoa: Wrong White Crowd' at Mahara Gallery, Waikanae, 2006. In this parody of early colonial
photographs the kuia wears **Aotearoa Coat of Arms**, a customised coat with antique button map,
Maori print scarf and bowler hat customised with a wool tie and feather trim (smoke: model's own).

Order *(left)* and Chaos
*(right) Working with triangles
in the kilim tradition in* Order
*became onerous, so Monika
Vance used her yarns like paint
brushes for the complementary*
Chaos, *to prove it can be
beautiful too.*

Monika Vance

In 1972, when handweaver Monika Vance first
came to New Zealand, she was horrified at the
lack of colour in the work of local weavers.

 thought, ooh! everything is brown.
And they were quite strict about how
you were allowed to weave — complex
looms were frowned on. There
weren't any colours and there weren't any fancy
yarns.'

For someone who loves colour it was a shock,
especially as Monika had come direct from
living in Thailand, where she was surrounded
by beautiful woven silks and cottons, and an
art school in Berlin where the students were
encouraged to try out new things 'left, right and
centre'.

The wool-only policy of the carpet industry,
where the industrial design-trained handweaver
was to work, was an introduction to another new
world. There were no carpet yarns that were not
wool — everything had to be natural. Rayon was

allowed, as a wood-based fibre, but Monika says,
'As a carpet yarn it's useless.' However, to see
twelve-foot-wide carpets coming off the tufting
machine with her design repeating over and over
was certainly exciting.

Thirty years on, much has changed. For
people working with fibres there's much more
to play with — especially linen and silk, but also
many combinations of artificial fibres.

Monika spent four and a half years
at Berlin's Staatliche Meisterschule für
Kunsthandwerk, followed by a practical weaving
placement in Poland. Monika didn't understand
the language and had to concentrate hard on
what she was doing, but she met the most famous
Polish weaver, Magdalena Abakanowicz, who had
her designs woven at the same factory.

Monika and her family then moved to

'To work on a design and see it produced on the factory floor is very exciting,' she says. 'You would sit at your desk and think about it and hand your design over to the weavers and they'd come back with a whole lot of samples in different colour combinations. There were some beautiful results and some happy accidents.'

Namibia, where there were no textiles of note but 'colours to dream about' — landscapes with purple hills and white sand in the desert evening light. 'I enjoyed myself so much just looking.'

Once in New Zealand, Monika designed machine-woven, jacquard labels — 'a very interesting job' — then moved to working on a grand scale for the carpet factory. After another stint with the label weavers she was hired by an upholstery manufacturer, again for her knowledge of jacquard weaving.

Now living in Kerikeri, Monika still finds designing the most important part of the whole weaving process. 'To work on a design and see it produced on the factory floor is very exciting,' she says. 'You would sit at your desk and think about it and hand your design over to the weavers and they'd come back with a whole lot of samples in different colour combinations. There were some beautiful results and some happy accidents.' While she would still love to do industrial design, she says there's no opening here for a freelancer. 'The corporates want to own their designers, you don't have a name. It's very sad.'

From creating samples for someone else to translate into huge lengths, she now works on a tapestry loom, using the simplest weave of all. 'I have no access to technology any more so the design matters very much, the colour and shape and construction.' Rather than the pictorial images many tapestry weavers choose, Monika likes geometric patterns, especially the triangles of *Autumn Leaves*, the inspiration for which came from a scrap of a magazine picture. 'They're very nice to weave, triangles, like on the old kilims; they are full of energy.'

Edelweiss (opposite) is one of a series of three works (with a fourth to come) depicting the alpine flowers beloved by her late mother, who enjoyed walking in the European mountains. *Order and Chaos* (page 209), which was hung at the 2005 Creative Fibre exhibition in Wellington, was the result of a long thinking process. Originally there was just the zigzag *Order*, which took a while to figure out how to do. Then Monika was 'so fed up with those zigzags — I wanted to do something free and easy. So I used the yarns like a paint brush in *Chaos*, just to prove it can be done — and that chaos can be beautiful too.'

Edelweiss, one of a series depicting the alpine flowers beloved of the weaver's mother.

Coming with her professional training, Monika was surprised to find weavers here were mainly self-taught, apart from some tutoring from overseas weavers whose influences can be detected after they have gone — people like Archie Brennan and Lynne Curran, both tapestry weavers. The annual seminar of the Professional Weavers' Network is an occasion to look forward to, and Monika is also on the committee organising the next Professional Weavers' Network national exhibition.

Time takes its toll on weavers — Monika can't weave like she used to, though t'ai chi helps. 'I couldn't go to work, run a household and weave four hours every evening as I used to,' she says. 'I do two or three hours in the day and I have to be careful, more aware of how to move around and be fit.

'Handweaving is a traditional trade. Not many people have the knowledge any more, yet all the new technology comes from the old basic principles. You wonder where all that knowledge goes. I'm doing my best to keep this craft alive.' ∎

Sue Wademan

VISITORS TO QUEENSTOWN COME
ACROSS SUE WADEMAN'S WORK
BEFORE THEY MEET HER IN PERSON
— THE LOCAL ARTIST'S *FOUR
SEASONS* 'TEXTILE PAINTINGS' HANG
IN THE TERMINAL OF THE TOWN'S
INTERNATIONAL AIRPORT.

My Piece of Paradise,
*depicting the view from
Sue's apartment, is in
the collection of Jane and
Bill Thompson, who have
collected Sue Wademan's
works since the artist moved
to Queenstown.*

It's about ten years now since Australian-born Sue Wademan's textile art career took off, but it has taken her a while to find her own special way of using fabric. Now her fabric collage landscapes hang in homes and public spaces around the resort town where she and her English husband Spike, a commercial illustrator specialising in boats and planes, moved to live six years ago. Many more works are in overseas collections.

Her first commissioned quilt, *Valley Light*, remains in the Katoomba Regional Library. It depicts the blues and greens of the Blue Mountains, outside Sydney, where Sue and Spike lived for thirteen years while they raised their three children.

Sue's first job after leaving school was as a graphic artist in an advertising agency in Sydney. 'I grew up with a lovely mentor, an artist who lived in our street. He, like all budding artists, started off in commercial art, so that's where I went too. It was supposed to be very lucrative.' Sue worked on layout and design, and became

'I'd always had an empathy with fabric — I loved it. I had collected heaps of it
for making something out of some day.'

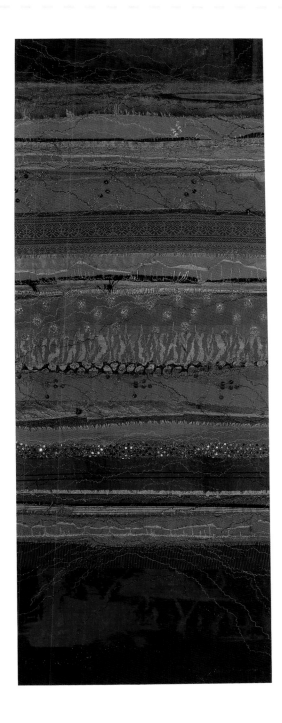

FAR LEFT: *Sue Wademan works in a studio in the heart of Queenstown.*

LEFT: **Red Merging** *is one of the 'soul work' landscapes for which she is best known.*

practised at working to a brief and meeting deadlines — all valuable lessons for her later career.

Once she had her children, Sue spent seven years on 'pottery, puppetry and sewing stretch knits' and also taught after-school art classes in Springwood, near Katoomba. She became interested in quilting through a friend, Yvonne Chapman, who used textiles in a particularly colourful way, and decided to go along to her patchwork group, the Blue Tongues. Learning by watching others, Sue began to experiment almost as soon as she started working in textiles. 'I'd always had an empathy with fabric — I loved it. I had collected heaps of it for making something out of some day.'

She sold one of her potter's wheels and bought a sewing machine. Her first quilt was a map of Australia, hand-pieced in tiny triangles, for the country's bicentennial — she took photos of it and others of this era to a workshop recently to show students she could actually make a quilt.

Sue went through several stages of influence — Amish, Japanese and early twentieth-century artists such as Klimt and Matisse — then signed up for a machine appliqué class with American Harriet Hargreaves, somewhat overcome by

The Kawarau River is 'the mighty river' that carves out the gorge leading into Queenstown. 'It's like the creative hand of God on the landscape.'

nerves at the thought of a highflying, overseas tutor. Her loving husband brought her home a 'super-duper' new machine as a surprise to take with her, but Sue didn't have a clue how to use it. Once she did, she leapt into her 'country cottage era' and made hundreds of appliquéd chook-and-pumpkin quilts to sell at her local market.

It was English textile artist, Celia Player, who showed Sue she could make art as well as geometric quilts, but she would need to learn how to do machine free-motion quilting first. The stitching 'paints' in the detail and holds

often-precious fabric scraps to the supporting canvas. That was 1994.

'Celia's workshop was a real breakthrough — the idea that I could interpret a picture with fabric and stitch was a revelation,' she says.

In 1996, Sue was selected to write a chapter in the book *Quilt Skills* (published by JB Fairfax) and to represent Australia at the Houston Quilt Market in the US, as a teacher, exhibitor and to promote the book. She had works included in exhibitions that toured to Japan and the US, with associated books that are still being sold

'As I look back, I've come full circle, with my love of fabric and
my love of art coming together in what I do.'

years afterwards. The first of her Uluru (Ayers Rock) works was in 'Colours of Australia', and there was another in 'Australia Dreaming', which resulted in an invitation to teach in eight cities in Japan — and although Sue had spent several years learning the Japanese language, she was still given an interpreter in class.

One thing continues to lead to another; Sue has now taught in more than ten countries — eight weeks around Europe, UK and Ireland in 2004 was her longest tour. Her work was included in *New Zealand Quilter* magazine's tour to Seattle and Birmingham in 2004, and it is regularly sold in a Santa Fe, New Mexico, gallery. Major commissions include work for a mansion in Jakarta, the Radisson Hotel foyer in Sydney and private homes in Queenstown.

The decision to come to New Zealand goes back to 1974, when the couple honeymooned in Queenstown, followed much later by visits during two teaching stints. 'The beauty of the landscape in and around Queenstown lured us here,' says Sue. 'We just fell in love with the thriving, affluent, spellbinding beauty of the place, and decided over a glass of champagne in the Wharf café on the edge of Lake Wakatipu

that we would find a way to come and live in Queenstown, New Zealand.'

And find a way they did. Returning earlier this year from a visit to Sydney to see her first grandchild, Sue feels a real sense of place as she flies over the snow-capped Remarkables into Queenstown. 'They say here that if you stick it out for seven years you will stay. We're coming up to our seventh winter — so I think we're staying!'

A consistent winner of regional art awards — Arrowtown Autumn Festival for four years, Wanaka, Oamaru and several Queenstown Arts Society awards — the well-focused Sue Wademan has secured her place in the local art scene. Her first New Zealand solo exhibition — a series of vineyard works — was in 2003 at the Mt Edward boutique winery, owned by art mentor and 'godfather of winemaking' Alan Brady.

Sue works most days from ten till six in her colourful studio in the old schoolhouse in the town centre, and is currently exhibiting her work locally in Queenstown's prestigious Ivan Clarke Gallery.

'As I look back, I've come full circle, with my love of fabric and my love of art coming together in what I do.' ∎

Deborah Walsh

WICKER OR WOOL, IT'S ALL THE SAME TO DEBORAH WALSH. THE NELSON ARTIST HAS DEMONSTRATED HER ABILITY TO CRAFT RECOGNISABLE SHAPES FROM WILLOW TWIGS, OLD BLANKETS — EVEN A SWANNDRI.

With four Mac's Nelson Sculpture Symposia under her belt, Deborah has previously worked in willow, kelp and flax. She has created hearts, tiki, deer and a larger-than-life portrait of a friend's dog from the natural materials. But in 2005, following the Kiwi culture theme she has pursued since starting her art degree, she made a tiki (opposite) from an olive-green Swannie. She originally thought she would use the Swanndri as a 'human cipher', perhaps as part of a series . . . then she tossed it on the ground. 'Then I looked at it and thought — goddammit, you're a tiki!' she says. Not wanting to cut into the garment any more than she had to, she folded and tucked and twisted and stitched until she had her fabric origami sculpture, which she called *Bush Tiki*. One of only two women at the annual gathering, which is held in the main street below the town's cathedral, she was determined her work should stand with the more traditional sculptors' hard materials — stone and wood.

Deborah, who insists she is no embroiderer, loves playing with woollen fabric. Her *Hokey Tikis* — little green or red felt brooches with contrasting red or green stitching and vintage buttons — sell like hotcakes at Nelson's Suter Gallery.

Deborah, who was born in Liverpool, came to Nelson as a seven-year-old. As a child she was an 'inveterate fiddler', and always enjoyed drawing and cartooning. In her thirties, while working as a chef — cooking was her creative outlet — she visited galleries and read about art, but never thought she could make it herself. When she wanted a year off cooking, she began a course at Nelson Polytechnic and stayed on.

Bush Tiki *was created at the Mac's Sculpture Symposium in Nelson in 2005.*

Huia Gun *uses tweed fabric, dressing gowns and swanndris from opportunity shops to comment on extinction.*

'I had a great time and came out the other end determined to be an artist.'

As a late starter, Deborah feels she benefited from having some world experience. Making a late change to jewellery in her last year at polytechnic, she applied the whole Kiwi 'she'll be right' attitude to her work — as long as it was wearable she wasn't too worried about technique. She became hooked on scrimshaw,

which gave her a 'nautical and sailorish way' of commenting on the first encounters between Cook and the Maori.

Moving to the Wairarapa, Deborah continued to work on her jewellery until a burglary left her with no tools, forcing her to use materials on hand. On the deer farm where she was living it was the right time of year to harvest

Huia Gun is wrapped in the kind of fabric the man who shot the last huia might have worn. 'He would have had a tweed jacket and woollen garments,' she says.

the pliable withies or willow shoots. 'I started out to make a wee willow ball, not knowing anything about it, and it got enormous!' Then she made a figure based on a character in the Hammer horror classic called *The Wicker Man* and called it Edward Woodward after the lead actor.

After a trip to the UK to study willow lore and meet basket makers, coming back to Nelson felt just like coming home. Deborah had a house to check up on, summer was kicking in . . . and she stayed on. Having a studio on her property near the port meant she could work full-time and 'just about manage' financially.

She has been collecting old blankets, travel rugs and tweed — preferably with labels intact — for some time. *Huia Gun* (opposite) is wrapped in the kind of fabric the man who shot the last huia might have worn. 'He would have had a

tweed jacket and woollen garments,' she says.

For the 2006 'Sonic' theme show at Sea Level sculpture gallery at Tasman, near Nelson, Deborah used what came to hand. A bulk lot of cow horns — a gift from a man who does home kills — became *Baffle* (beads made from the outer horns, threaded on steel cable) with the coral-like core wrapped once more in blankets and entitled *Stifle*. Deborah also made a soft fur speech bubble — *Hush;* and *Muffle* — sushi roll bullseye forms of vintage furs.

Deborah's 'perverse mission' is to be ranked alongside traditional sculptors working in hard materials. It's part of her ongoing protest at the ghettoisation of women's work. 'You have to prove it to yourself first, then prove it to the world.' ∎

Gwen Wanigasekera

STUDYING FOR A MASTERS DEGREE IN ANTHROPOLOGY HAS BEEN BOTH FRUSTRATING AND REWARDING FOR HAMILTON QUILTER GWEN WANIGASEKERA. TAKING TIME OUT FROM QUILTING IS HARD FOR THIS COMPULSIVE STITCHER, WHOSE WORK HANGS IN PUBLIC SPACES SUCH AS THE WAIKATO MUSEUM OF ART AND HISTORY, MANUKAU POLYTECHNIC AND WAIKATO UNIVERSITY'S LANGUAGE INSTITUTE AND SCHOOL OF LAW.

Silks, satins, velvets and wools are pieced over papers in the English tradition to make large quilts such as Time Piece *(opposite).*

want to make quilts, as well as write,' she says, 'but I do love to study. I enjoy it immensely'. Gwen has been researching her thesis, in 'anthropology with an art history bias', for the last year. She interviewed quilters around the country, finding out what part their work plays in their lives.

'I was trying to untangle some of the ideas about art and the way it's commodified,' she says, 'the way it is thought about differently by different groups of people — what it means to them. I have been particularly interested in the way that objects made by women are used, viewed and thought about.'

While she very much enjoyed the unusual opportunity of getting to know all the people she interviewed, as a quilter she found it frustrating being immersed in the quilting world and not having much time to make her own quilts.

One of New Zealand's earliest converts to quilting, before the renaissance around the US bicentennial celebrations in 1976, Gwen discovered it in the simplest of ways. Married and living in Britain in the early seventies, she began making up Cloth Kits, those cut-on-the-dotted-line garments that simplified the sewing process for a new generation of novice dressmakers. They also provided an 'alternative'

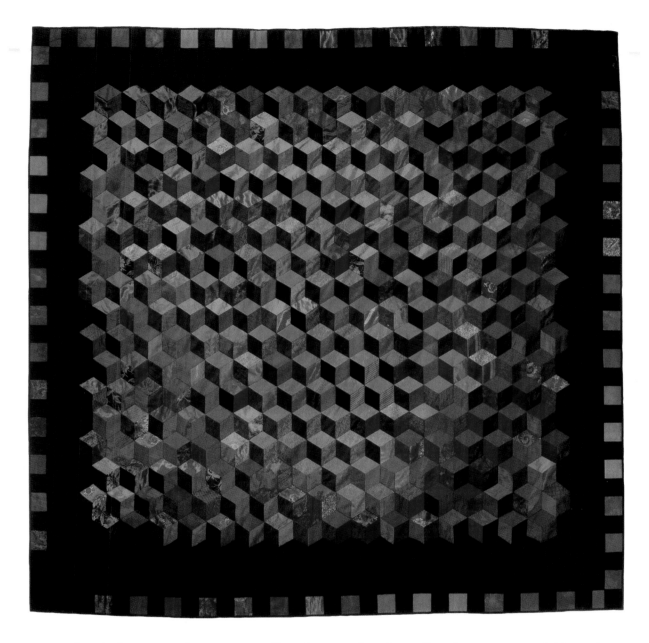

style with their original screen-printed lengths of cloths. 'I hadn't ever done quilting, but there were lines marked on the fabric where you had to machine quilt. I loved the sculptural effect so I just had to keep going.'

She then learned to hand-stitch over papers in the English method of patchwork, and still does a lot of that kind of traditional piecing —

though usually in less conventional fabrics than the cottons of Jane Austen's day, when it was the fashion for young women to aim for precision in handwork.

Now, as light relief from writing, a box of thirties cotton fabrics, already tacked over long hexagon-shaped papers sits at the end of Gwen's large coffee table, beside orderly piles of colour-tabbed library books on every aspect of textile production and women's work. A project that started with a legacy discovered in her grandmother's treadle sewing machine — 'There was a whole lot of old fabric rolled up inside!' — English piecing the hexagons should satisfy her itch to stitch, at least until the thesis is finished.

'I do a lot of traditional patchwork. I like the structure of it and the formality of it, and then the surprises as secondary patterns emerge. I do other things as well, but I go back to it.'

Although she had made patchwork, she had never quilted until she married. Gwen became aware of fabric as a young child growing up in the area known as Moonlight, in the Grey Valley, a long strip of land with a history of sawmilling and goldmining. 'My grandmother was a teacher at the school, which was started by my great-grandfather. Both she and my mother were also postmistresses — the post office was in our backyard.' The school — which often had only about ten children, as it did when Gwen started there — was closed in 2004. Her feelings about

that are memorialised in the blackboard-sized quilt *Ink*, which incorporates the words 'Requiem for a country school'. Old linen in various shades of that dark greenish-blue used both for blackboards and bulk supplies for school inkpots are pieced together as a surface on which to write her message in white fabric paint.

Gwen can vividly remember textures and colours from when she was little. 'I was really fascinated with the lining fabrics in men's suits, where you get two colours changing — I think it was called shot silk.' It's an effect she has often emulated in her traditionally pieced work, where she uses subtle gradations of colour and texture to give that 'shot' look, so that light moves over the work in unexpected ways. No purist when it comes to fibre, she will combine cotton, linen, velvets, wools, rayon and silk from whatever source. She still collects old ties — not necessarily silk — and knows every op-shop in the Waikato district.

Some of Gwen's most powerful memories as a child were of her family's annual pilgrimage from the West Coast to Christchurch's Robert

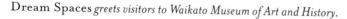

Dream Spaces greets visitors to Waikato Museum of Art and History.

Ink, *pieced from old linen, memorialises country schools.*

McDougall Art Gallery and Canterbury Museum. 'The museum and art gallery were wonderful places that caught our imagination. Today I still visit museums — to be inspired, sometimes challenged, to see things of the past and possibly of the future. The museum is still a place to imagine.'

The chance to visit museums in Britain and research historical collections came courtesy of a Queen Elizabeth II Arts Council grant in 1991, when she spent five weeks there. 'I saw amazing work, often visiting the museums' storage facilities — they were real treasure houses.'

Dream Spaces, the work that greets visitors to the Waikato Museum of Art and History in Hamilton, arose from the concept of the space in museums between the viewer and the object. 'It is in this space we may see or place ourselves,'

Gwen says. The work is made up of five quilts, assembled like a carved lintel at the threshold to a wharenui. 'It both welcomes you at the entrance and is a marker of that entrance and the signalling of entering a new space.' Gwen sees *Dream Spaces* as 'very Waikato' — using Waikato colours and being pieced out of triangles.

Gwen Wanigasekera continues to alternate between personal pieces, often assembled by machine, and handpieced and often very large and geometric works in a variety of rich fabrics. 'I've always loved geometry, it was the one piece of maths I understood really well. You're supposed to work in series, I know, but I work more in overlapping spirals,' she says. 'There's the life spiral and the pattern spiral, and just occasionally those two elements are present in the same quilt.' ■

Jewel of the Pacific *incorporates blue and turquoise Pacific hues.*

Donna Ward

DREAMING OF HAWAII IS THE TITLE OF ONE OF DONNA WARD'S QUILTS, AND IT PERFECTLY SUMS UP HER VIBRANT PACIFIC QUILTING STYLE. BUT DONNA IS ALSO AN AWARD-WINNING TEACHER.

onna, who is known for her sparkling sense of fun and *joie de vivre*, loves teaching. In fact, she is so good at it she was given an international award in recognition. The Jewel Pearce Patterson Scholarship for International Quilt Teachers allowed her to exhibit her work and attend workshops in 2003 at the acclaimed Houston Quilt Market and Festival in the US.

She has also had her quilts widely exhibited in New Zealand, Australia, France, the UK and the US, and is hard pressed to choose between teaching and making her quilts, which are known for their simple shapes and eye-popping colour. 'I've always had a fascination with Hawaiian quilts but never wanted to do them by hand,' Donna says. 'Without even realising it I was strongly affected by the patterns. I was subconsciously developing it — purely for the love of it.'

Rather than the hand appliqué and quilting that characterise traditional Hawaiian work, however, Donna machine appliqués these on her 'trusty Husky' (the sewing machine supplied to her by manufacturer Husqvarna in recognition of her success) and she machine quilts using decorative threads. The large, blue and turquoise *Dreaming of Hawaii* took the Best of Country prize from 32 invited New Zealand quilts at the 2001 World Quilt on Tour show in the US. *Jewel of the Pacific* (opposite) is her latest large work.

When precision piecing is necessary, Donna uses foundation piecing (over a marked paper), in quilts such as *Hot Summer Beauty* (page 229), based on the traditional New York Beauty block.

Although Donna began quilting in a traditional way, she now works entirely by machine — not surprising, given that she had her own machine at the age of seven, working alongside her mother, a dressmaker by trade. 'It

'I love teaching the most — people sometimes do incredible things they didn't know they could do. They challenge me a lot! I pick the ones who need a push. Some fabulous results have happened.'

was a gorgeous little Singer my mother bought for me. It was a toy made of metal, but it did a chain stitch and if the power went off my mum would grab my machine and keep sewing!'

Donna acquired a 'bigger but basic' electric Singer before she was even at high school, and sewed her own clothes. She was making her own quilts before she left school 'because all I had to use was Mum's old scraps'.

Now it's her turn to talk to school kids about making quilts. Donna works out of a new studio and retail shop on former railway land in Frankton, Hamilton, and her 16-year-old daughter, Ashleigh, helps out in the shop. At the new premises in Railside Place — strangely enough, in the street where Donna once lived in a railway house and in space converted from the workshops where her husband did his apprenticeship — there's plenty of room, for classes and her own work, as well as the fabric for which she's known. Before moving in, Donna worked in the 'old baby room' at her home for around 20 years.

She loves to use bright, clear colour, not distinctively patterned — batik fabric is a favourite — and although she has had a go at dyeing her own fabric she's not good at it. In spite of thinking she would stock a range for all tastes in Donna's Quilt Studio, customers tell her the fabric definitely reflects her own taste.

'People come in knowing what I like and find it here,' she says.

One of the founders of the Waikato Patchworkers and Quilters Guild, as a novice quilter, Donna didn't plan her business venture. The opportunity of space came up and she took it, mostly as a way of continuing her teaching career. A medical receptionist since school, working in intensive care, Donna always thought she might retrain as a nurse. However, as her interest in quilting snowballed and things got 'out of control' at home, she became more involved in teaching others. 'I would put my son Luke to sleep then start teaching night classes at the local high school.' With adult education classes under threat for various reasons, she could see herself losing that opportunity.

Now taking seven classes a week and teaching at weekends as well, Donna sees herself as a personal trainer. With a teaching style that emphasises enjoyment, pleasure and fun, there are no rules in her classes, only guidelines. 'I love teaching the most — people sometimes do incredible things they didn't know they could do. They challenge me a lot! I pick the ones who need a push. Some fabulous results have happened.'

In her own recent work, the colours and patterns of the Pacific prevail — tapa cloth patterns and the natural environment: leaves,

flowers, small sprigs and ferns. Donna is now feeling somehow at a crossroads and not quite sure what she will do next. She likes to have a big project to work on.

'It may take ages, I don't mind. With all this fabric at my fingertips, once I get over all that business stuff I think I'll put up something huge.' ■

Hot Summer Beauty *updates the traditional New York Beauty block in midsummer colours.*

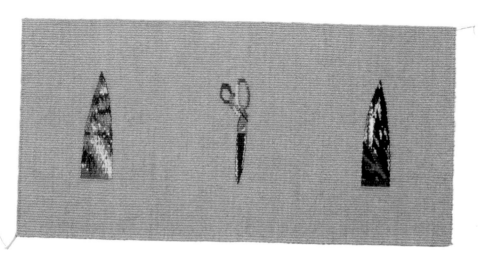

Kate Wells

KATE WELLS IS NOT AN ARTIST
WHO LIVES IN SPLENDID ISOLATION.
SHE IS FULLY INVOLVED IN HER
COMMUNITY AS A CURATOR, TUTOR,
DESIGNER AND ART PROJECT
CO-ORDINATOR — AS WELL AS
A MOTHER OF SCHOOL-AGE
CHILDREN.

 ate, a tapestry weaver, made her mark with the 1990 'Fish Out of Water' exhibition which toured public galleries around New Zealand. Themes and motifs in those fifteen tapestries — islands, fish and the sea — were to resurface over a decade later in the 2005 woven tapestry and découpage panel series *The Hunt: A Medieval Antipodean Offshore Odyssey* (opposite and page 235), which toured nationally through to July 2006.

Based on the famous medieval Unicorn Tapestries in the Metropolitan Museum of Art in New York, Kate's interpretation also uses allegory, in this case to reflect contemporary concerns about New Zealand's natural resources in the face of changing attitudes and values.

Currently relishing the role of curator at Lopdell House Gallery in Titirangi, Auckland, Kate has in the last few years acted as lead artist on several civic and community projects, the most recent of which is the Auckland Regional Council's Botanic Gardens Visitor Centre, Huakaiwaka, which took a 2005 Creative Places Award.

Closer to home, Kate has been contracted

TOP TO BOTTOM:
The Hunt: Propagation;
The Hunt: Tide 1;
The Hunt: Tide 2.

as lead artist for several major Waitakere City Council projects, under their enlightened policy of contracting artists onto design teams at the beginning of all new building projects. In 2002, Massey Leisure Centre and Library took the New Zealand Creative Places Award. As lead artist, Kate identified themes and materials in order to co-ordinate the design of the complex inside and out. She commissioned work from artists such as Fatu Feu'u and Jeff Thomson, and contributed several of her own designs, including two made by Christchurch firm Dilana Rugs. *Riding on the Unicorn's Back* is a rug for

children to roll on in the library, and *Pathways* a carpet runner. Drawing on her initial research into the area's history and flora, the runner depicts a pathway from the Waitakere foothills, through the trees and kauri gum fields to the shores of the Waitemata, evoking a sense of place and past.

Born in Foxton in 1961, Kate was knitting at the age of four and weaving at seven, so going on to study textile design at Wellington Polytechnic in 1981 was a natural progression. Two decades later, she completed a Master of Fine Arts at Elam, University of Auckland. In between, there

ABOVE: The Hunt:
Keepers and Watchers.

LEFT: *Kate Wells in her
studio gallery 'Breaksea' at
Titirangi.*

were some major artistic milestones: the 'Art
of Knitting' exhibition at The Dowse, 1984,
featuring one-off knitted jerseys; 'Birdland',
1986 at The Dowse; 'No Man's Land', 1992,
and inclusion in the 'Under Southern Skies'
exhibition of New Zealand textiles at London's
Barbican Centre in 1996.

Much of Kate's inspiration comes from
the bush — there are eight mature kauri trees
on 'Breaksea', the property where she lives with
her partner Simon Grant, a writer, and their
children Oscar and Imogen. Kate and Simon
have collaborated on writing three children's

books, with her drawings illustrating his stories.
Kate's studio, built onto the front of an existing
weatherboard house, has polished wooden floors
that are perfect for displaying the large tufted
rugs that Kate designs and Dilana Rugs makes.

The Hunt, for which Kate received a Creative
New Zealand new works grant, is like the
original Unicorn Tapestries in that it tells stories
— New Zealand stories of natural resources and
their vulnerability: small coastal islands where
introduced animals such as the goat vie for space
with endangered plants like *Tecomanthe speciosa*; where
marine reserves are encroached on by real estate
developments, and where quarantine stations
isolate the unwanted. Kate says, 'I am interested in
the ironies and ambiguities in our history and how
beliefs and values can alter over time.'

In her catalogue essay, Felicity Milburn
concludes: 'Repeating patterns, connecting
threads, coded symbols and overlapping layers
are all characteristic of the ancient art of tapestry
but they also reflect the nature of storytelling
across the ages, which offers the potential for
new interpretations, changing meanings and a
slightly different ending every time.' ■

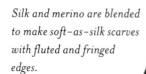

Silk and merino are blended to make soft-as-silk scarves with fluted and fringed edges.

Tracy White

TRACY WHITE KNOWS EVERY PART OF THE WOOL FIBRE PROCESS FROM SHEARING TO FINISHED PRODUCT. IN HER FIBRE STUDIO IN THE OLD MAILROOM OF THE FORMER WOODVILLE POST OFFICE, NEXT DOOR TO THE POLICE STATION, SHE TURNS WOOL, ALPACA AND SILK INTO RAINBOW-HUED SLIVERS FOR SPINNERS, KNITTERS, WEAVERS AND FELTERS.

'The fibre is never going to be the main focus, and with winters of between 30 and 50 degrees below zero it's no wonder the raw product has many degrees of fault.'

She deals with mountains of raw product, has her own dyeing cookhouse — which doubles as the smoko room — and even accommodates the odd commercial knitting machine, left over from the heyday of New Zealand's wool textile industry. Affectionately known as Woolville, the studio is an 'avalanche zone,' she says, 'and that lovely pile represents a huge amount of work!'

Since 2002 Tracy has chosen to focus on making felt. That year, she travelled to Mongolia as one of four volunteers teaching a group of women skills to improve their lives, as well as those of their families and villages. Each tutor had a specialist topic — knitting, spinning, dyeing or felting, which was Tracy's.

It was quite a responsibility, she says. 'Every step of their lives is long, slow and often difficult and sometimes life-threatening. I already knew they were nomadic and often lived in felt huts (called *ger* by the Mongolians), and I was apprehensive about the fact they needed someone from the other side of the world to show them how to make felt.'

Nothing is wasted in Mongolian life. Not only do their animals grow the fibre, but they are eaten and milked, their skins are tanned and even dung is utilised. 'The fibre is never going to be the main focus, and with winters of between 30 and 50 degrees below zero it's no wonder the raw product has many degrees of fault.'

After living a rather nomadic life herself, from childhood into her twenties, Tracy is pleased to be putting down roots, with somewhere to lay not just her head but stow all the stored stuff she has collected over the years — a couple spent at Victoria University, which introduced her to tramping and a lifelong 'fibre friend' who was then screenprinting luminous lycra tights for rock climbers; three more spent at Wellington Polytech's textile design diploma course that taught her to spin, felt, weave and dye; a couple of years working as a rouseabout in a shearing shed at Nelson Lakes, and a one-year wool technology diploma at Massey, learning everything she could about our national fibre.

Trips overseas — including a shearing season in Norway and four months on a sheep and wool studying scholarship in the UK — showed her how other countries grow and process wool. On her return she fell in love with merino wool while shearing the super-fine fleeces.

Ruffled edges on a fine silk and merino scarf.

Tracy's memories of felt in the early nineties were of coarse material like stiff cardboard, but with her newly acquired access to lovely fine merino fibre, she has gone to the other end of the scale. Blending silk with merino has produced whisper-fine soft-as-silk scarves and wraps that drape like no traditional felt ever did, and she continues to develop the fluted and fringed edgings that have become her signature. Now she has discovered Suri Alpaca, the ultimate in fibres in many people's opinions.

Her work is now sold in New Zealand and overseas, and she has won several awards at national Creative Fibre festivals, Opotiki Fibre and Fleece, and Blenheim's Textile Fantasia exhibitions.

With a certificate in adult teaching from Palmerston North's UCOL, Tracy travels the country tutoring for creative fibre and embroidery groups. 'I really like to work in solitude,' she says. 'I could easily become a recluse! Then my strong practical, logical side kicks in. I try to maintain this mad reclusive urge and balance it with human contact in the form of tutoring. That exhausts me, yet my students without exception continuously inspire me. There is as much learning done on my part as the students'. My workbook gets a thrashing after a class, noting down things to try myself at a later date!'

Tracy's shearing and pig-hunting partner Willy, and his half dozen dogs, give her life a much-needed balance. 'The novelty of the transient lifestyle wore off. I've bought myself a humble little state house and it's my heaven.' However, she says, a day in the shearing shed every so often is very grounding. 'I sleep soundly and wake with a fresh mind and body. I have a sense of value in actually working hard for a return simply because I can.

'Feltmaking is literally as old as the hills — it's been made for 3000 years they say, and here it is still being made and modified and titivated. It's historical, it's hands-on, it's relatively quick to do, it's not an exclusive activity, it's explorative, it's able to be done by anyone, not just those with money. It's not just about survival anymore.' ■

Suri alpaca produces whisper-soft felt with superb draping qualities.

*Pacific influences are evident
in Mandy Wilson's rugs.*

Mandy Wilson

MANDY WILSON'S RUGS ARE MADE FOR WALKING ON. THE DEEP PILE INVITES YOU TO CURL YOUR TOES INTO IT. HER DESIGNS ARE UNDERSTATED — A HINT OF PASIFIKA, THE SUGGESTION OF STONES, FLOWERS AND SHELL FORMS, SUBTLE COLOURS WITH ENOUGH WARMTH TO COUNTERACT MINIMALIST INTERIORS AND COMPLEMENT CONTEMPORARY ART.

nlike the knotted rugs of the seventies which adorned walls, Mandy Wilson's wool rugs are strictly for underfoot, perfect for floors stripped to the bare boards or polished concrete. They're functional, hardwearing, to be used and loved. 'As floor coverings I hope my rugs are challenging,' she says. 'They are not intended to be walked over and ignored!'

Working with a heavy-duty, air-fired tufting gun takes muscle power, which is why Mandy's slight build comes as a surprise. And the work of handling her thick tufted wool floor rugs, once off the frame, helps build stamina.

A carpet design graduate from Kidderminster College at England's Midlands University, Mandy fell in love with the tufting process in her third year at university, on a work experience placement. Even though it's tough work physically and very laborious — and tufted rugs were unusual back in the early eighties — after the first few minutes with the tufting gun Mandy knew this was what she wanted to do. She is still doing it, 20 years later.

After some years working in the British design industry for Designers Guild and Helen Yardley Rugs, Mandy came out to New Zealand in 1997 with her Kiwi husband Glenn and began making rugs part-time when sons James and Henry were little. For the past five years, she has worked three to four days a week during school hours at the House of Rugs, on Wellington's Thorndon Quay, surrounded by imported carpets and her own rugs. There's space to store a stock of carpet yarns, though not the colour range she could once get, especially since traditional multi-coloured, patterned Axminsters are no longer popular. She says she would never dye her own wool; 'It's really important for quality control that the carpet

Sculpted surfaces provide interest in Mandy Wilson's newest work, right and opposite.

yarn is dyed professionally.'

The design is drawn onto the reverse of a strong, polypropylene base cloth stretched over a large vertical wooden frame. Following her outlines, Mandy creates a pile by shooting loops of yarn from the back through to the front with a gun resembling a power drill fitted with a specialised needle and blade. Only a skewed view of the pile face is visible while she's working, as the frame is set half a metre from the building's side wall, to allow plenty of room on the working side. When it's finished, the stitches are latexed and a backing glued on before the top of the pile is sheared and the edges hand trimmed.

While most of the rugs Mandy makes for the shop are a standard size of 1400 x 2000 mm, she also works to commission — anything from long hall runners, circles, squares and rectangular rugs of up to 2500 x 3000 mm. It can take up to 50 hours to make a rug, depending on size — 'Five to eight weeks, depending on how busy I am' — and the colours in her work come to life, often taking on a new radiance, after it has been shorn with a kind of handheld lawnmower. In some of her recent work Mandy has sculpted the surface, leaving a circle to stand up above the lower pile.

Inspired by all sorts of textiles, and the designs and colours of many twentieth-century artists, Mandy especially loves Henri Matisse for his purity of line, decorative pattern and colour. Her own designs are evocative rather than pictorial, inspired by eternal and organic images — pebbles or driftwood from the Eastbourne beach near her home, a full stop, lines which link the past to the present. Whether spirals, seeds or simply circles, 'Aesthetically beautiful symbols each have their own story to reveal,' she says.

Now she has lived here a while, she has developed a Pacific influence in her designs, but she uses a more European colour palette — 'Interesting neutrals with touches of bright colour.

'My ideal commission is when the client says, "I really love what you do, I would like a rug, so big, in these sorts of colours, I'll leave it to you to come up with something really stunning."' ■

Untitled — I am
travelling through
submerged lands.

Esther Woollaston

THE PALEST BLUES, BEIGES, MAUVES AND MINT GREENS MERGE IN
CALMING BLENDS OF SOFT COTTON AND LINEN LIKE THE WATERS OF
WELLINGTON ON A STILL, GREY DAY. SYMBOLS FLOAT TO THE SURFACE
OCCASIONALLY, HAND QUILTING MEANDERS ACROSS THE SURFACE LIKE
WATER AT LOW TIDE, TO LINK THE LAYERS WITH TINY, EVEN STITCHES.
PATTERN, IF ANY, IS MUTED, BARELY THERE.

Esther Woollaston's quilts emanate serenity. Subtle, ethereal, cool and quiet — somewhat like the quiltmaker herself, who overlooks the harbour from her hillside Brooklyn home — they are stitched from recycled fabrics softened by age and use, chosen deliberately for their patina and sheer oldness. Most are pastel, fresh yet subtle, though some earlier works used deeper blues and purples.

Esther's quilts work beautifully with today's minimalist interiors, though that is the last thing on her mind. Not one for clutter, she herself seems to float quietly among her belongings.

'There are so many memories, like someone's left a little bit of themselves in the fabric,' she says. 'And there's a satisfaction in making something lovely out of plain ordinary bits of material.' Esther uses old fabrics sourced from op-shops and fairs because it's softer and easier to work with than new — an important consideration when it comes to hand-quilting layers of cloth.

A quilter since 1985, when she made a cushion with her father's ties and discovered she was patchworking, Esther came to fame nationally in 2000 as the winner of the inaugural Pataka Millennium Award for Excellence in Quiltmaking, a choice that generated much discussion at the time.

This was the first national exhibition in a public art museum, where quilts must be judged by criteria more usually applied to visual art, and there are no extra points for complex piecing and fancy quilting. The simplicity of *Niches* was stunning — judge and art curator at

The Deep Underground
Pear Tree Avenue *comes from
'a very deep place that I go to
occasionally'.*

Pataka, Helen Kedgley, described it as having 'an emotional quality, a spiritual quality.

'She's looking within and using colour and shape to create something that speaks to people. There's a quietness about it — it has a subtle beauty, ethereal colours, a sense of frailty. It's a traditional quilt but it's her own artistic statement.'

Esther's love of colour and form goes back to her childhood on an isolated dairy farm in Taranaki — also the home territory of her uncle Toss Woollaston — and her work is still influenced by that setting. 'My birthplace had a really strong effect,' she says. 'It was a formidable landscape, lush, rugged and very powerful.'

Not much bright colour there — just the greens and browns of the bush and grass, swede and carrot crops. It's not surprising that when she started school, Esther had a strong reaction to the brightly coloured blocks of the infant classroom.

As a child she loved dolls, stitching clothes for them from scraps, and making oven cloths at school from sacking and wool. Her grandmother taught her to embroider and knit. However, as a left-hander she preferred hand-stitching — her mother was too busy to teach her to use the sewing machine and at school she spent half a year unpicking a machine-stitched apron.

One of Esther's earliest memories is of watching a huge yellow and black bumble bee climbing into a red runner bean flower. She also remembers fabrics from her childhood. 'I vividly remember one particular fabric with leaves on it and a silky dress with rosebuds and smocking.' Those memories are touched on in her 'weekend quilts' — *joie de vivre* things, based on traditional patterns but still easily identifiable as Esther Woollaston quilts — that she makes between her abstract, minimalist works. 'I like the way the emotive quilts come up to the surface between other quilts,' she says.

The Deep Underground Pear Tree Avenue (opposite) is one of the meditative quilts that come from 'a very deep place that I go to occasionally'. *Untitled — I Am Travelling Through Submerged Lands* (page 243) is the sort of landscape where a journey past a landmark like Mana Island often reflects what is happening inside the traveller.

Esther is one of very few quilters who will take on hand-quilting assignments for other patchworkers, who haven't the time or space for the time-consuming work on the frame. She finds quilting such an enjoyable process that if she has nothing of her own on the go — and there are usually half a dozen quilts at different stages — she is happy to do work for friends. And because it's such an organic process all sorts of ideas come through as she stitches. ∎

'My birthplace had a really strong effect,' she says. 'It was a formidable landscape, lush, rugged and very powerful.'

Contact details

Mieke Apps
25 Mawson Avenue
RD2
Kerikeri (by appt only)
phone: +64 9 407 3395
website: www.spectrumfabric.co.nz

Victoria Bell
email: hibiscusvictoria@clear.net.nz

Freda Brierley
email: fredabrierley@xtra.co.nz

Susan Broad
79 Albert Street
St Clair
Dunedin
phone: +64 3 455 0625
email: broboss@clear.net.nz

Rebecca Brown Thompson
phone: +64 3 337 8053
email: botanical@xtra.co.nz
website: www.rbrown.co.nz

Andrea Chandler
33 Queen's Road
Port Hills
Nelson

Lindy Chinnery
The Textile Emporium & Weaving Studio
9 Ross Place
Lawrence
Otago
phone: +64 3 485 9095
email: linjo5@kol.co.nz

Vita Cochran
email: vitaflora@hotmail.com

Cheryl Comfort
email: curator@quiltgallery.co.nz
website: www.quiltgallery.co.nz

Jane Coughlan
PO Box 101938
North Shore Mail Centre
Auckland
phone: +64 9 4424299
email: janecoughlan@ihug.co.nz
website: www.janecoughlan.com

Morag Dean
112 Long Plain Road
Anatoki RD1
Takaka 7183
phone: +64 3 525 7425
email: morag.dean@xtra.co.nz

Andrea du Chatenier
email: aduchatenier@paradise.net.nz

Anne Field
Studio at The Arts Centre
Worcester Boulevard
Christchurch
email: afield@chch.planet.org.nz
website: www.annefield.co.nz

Maree Garstang
'Karearea', RD8
Masterton 5888

Merrilyn George
58a Miro Street
Ohakune
email: kapai2@xtra.co.nz

Chelsea Gough
128 Main Street
Greytown

Jacqui Greenbank
email: jacgreenbank@hotmail.com

Bronwyn Griffiths
22 Maire Street
Eastbourne
Wellington

Katya Gunn
PO Box 5639
Dunedin
phone: +64 3 477 9944
email: katya@lucellan.com

Megan Hansen-Knarhoi
website: www.mrhk.co.nz

Anna Bibby Gallery
2 Morgan Street
Newmarket
Auckland
phone: +64 9 302 2599
email: annabibby@xtra.co.nz

Mary Newton Gallery
150 Vivian Street
Wellington
phone: +64 4 385 1699
website: www.marynewtongallery.com

Heather Harding
56 Longfellow Street
Upper Hutt

Malcolm Harrison
c/- Janne Land Gallery
Unit 1, 13 Jessie Street
Wellington
phone: +64 4 384 2912
website: www.janneland.co.nz

Susan Holmes
20 Ranch Avenue
Beach Haven
Auckland

Laura Hudson
412 Ruahine Street
Palmerston North
phone: +64 6 356 2385
email: lmv.hudson@inspire.net.nz

Janice Jones
40 Kennedy Crescent
Wanaka
phone: +64 3 443 7567
email: carrick.j@xtra.co.nz

Retail outlet:
Perendale Wool Shop
10 Helwick Street
Wanaka
phone: +64 3 443 7294

Laurel Judd
32 Trigg Crescent
Taradale
Napier
phone: +64 6 8448621
email: knitz@laurel.co.nz
website: www.laurel.co.nz

Heeni Kerekere
11 Fergusson Street
Huntly
phone: +64 27 525 4650 (mobile)
email: heeni.kerekere@twoa.ac.nz

Ming Wei Li
phone: +64 21 791 214 (mobile)
email: mingwei1234@gmail.com

Robin McLaughlin
10 Pleasant Place
Dunedin
phone: +64 3 473 9939
email: glenora@paradise.net.nz

Rosemary McLeod
PO Box 958
Wellington

Barbara McQuarrie
21 Weenink Road
Greymouth 7805
email: b_mcquarrie@minidata.co.nz

Serena McWilliam
email: serenamcw@paradise.net.nz

Lani Morris
16 Alpers Terrace
Napier
phone: +64 6 843 8740
email: lanimorris@xtra.co.nz

Katherine Morrison
84 Blue Mountains Road
Pinehaven
Hutt Valley
email:cmorris@nz1.ibm.com

Juliet Novena Sorrel
8 Kilgour Street
Seacliff
Otago
email: birdseyeview@paradise.net.nz

Genevieve Packer
website: www.curious.gen.nz

Robyn Parker
phone: +64 4 234 8983
email: robyn_parker@xtra.co.nz

Diana Parkes
31 Gurney Road
Lower Hutt 5010
phone: +64 4 565 0544
email: diana@dianaparkes.co.nz

Clare Plug
email: plugac@paradise.net.nz

Anna Prussing
PO Box 50065
Porirua

Marilyn Rea-Menzies
PO Box 13587
Christchurch
email: marilyn@tapestry.co.nz
website: www.tapestry.co.nz

Monique Redmond
email: percy@clear.net.nz

Jocelyn Seccombe
70 Vogel Street
Palmerston North 4414
phone: +64 6 359 0838
email: Jfseccombe@free.net.nz
email: Textileartist@gmail.com

Ailie Snow
23 Woodside Crescent
St Heliers
Auckland
email: ailie@paradise.net.nz

Sonia Snowden
email: ssnowden@xtra.co.nz

Sue Spigel
P O Box 7159
Christchurch
email: suespigel@xtra.co.nz

Yanny Split
PO Box 268
Huntly
phone: +64 7 828 9914
email: yanny@huntly.net.nz
website: www.huntly.net.nz

Suzanne Tamaki
Box 133
Otaki
email: nativesista@xtra.co.nz

Monika Vance
PO Box 616
Kerikeri 0245
email: monikavance@xtra.co.nz

Sue Wademan
PO Box 8
Queenstown
email: wademan@xtra.co.nz

Deborah Walsh
51 Mt Pleasant Avenue
Nelson
email: weevil@ihug.co.nz

Gwen Wanigasekera
email: gdwh@ihug.co.nz

Donna Ward
8B Railside Place
Frankton
Hamilton
phone: +64 7 847 3692
website: www.donnasquiltstudio.co.nz

Kate Wells
email: kate@clear.net.nz

Tracy White
94 Vogel Street
Woodville 4920
Tararua
email: tracywhite@inspire.net.nz

Mandy Wilson
c/- House of Rugs
141 Thorndon Quay
Wellington
phone: +64 4 499 1929
mobile: +64 27 242 6794
email: mandywilson@clear.net.nz

Esther Woollaston
email: estherw@paradise.net.nz

Image credits

Photography of works by Croydon Studios, photography of artists by Joanna Caird and copyright Random House/the artist except for the following:

pages 17, 19: courtesy Victoria Bell, photography by Ross Coombes.

pages 26–29: courtesy Rebecca Brown Thompson

pages 34, 36, 38, 39: courtesy Andrea du Chatenier

pages 80, 83: courtesy Jacquelyn Greenbank and 64zero3 Gallery, Christchurch

pages 98–102: courtesy Malcolm Harrison

page 105: 1996 World of Wearable Art Awards, 'Dragon Fish' by Susan Holmes, Auckland, courtesy World of Wearable Art Ltd.

page 106: 2003 World of Wearable Art Awards, 'Blue Lagoon' by Susan Holmes, Auckland, courtesy World of Wearable Art Ltd.

page 107: 2005 Montana World of Wearable Art Awards, 'Cage of Thorns' by Susan Holmes, Auckland, courtesy World of Wearable Art Ltd.

pages 117–118: courtesy Laurel Judd, photography by Kevin Bridle

pages 125–127: courtesy Ming Wei Li and Massey University, photography by Mark Coote

pages 134–135: courtesy Rosemary McLeod and Bowen Galleries

page 156: courtesy Genevieve Packer and The Dowse, Lower Hutt, photography by Mark Marriott

pages 165, 166, 169: courtesy Clare Plug, photography by Clive Ralph

page 170: courtesy Anna Prussing, photography by Larry Jordan

page 172: courtesy *New Zealand Quilter Magazine*, photograph by Helen Mitchell

page 175: courtesy Anna Prussing, photography by Larry Jordan

pages 182–183: courtesy Monique Redmond

pages 190–191: courtesy Ailie Snow

page 197 (top): courtesy Juliet Novena Sorrel, photography by M. Littlejohn

pages 198–199: courtesy Sue Spigel, photography by Melody Waltz Callahan

page 207: courtesy Suzanne Tamaki, photography by Greg Semu

page 224: courtesy Waikato Museum, gift of Friends of Waikato Museum

page 230: courtesy Kate Wells, photography by Faye Norman

page 233: courtesy Kate Wells, photography by Faye Norman

page 243: courtesy Esther Woollaston, photography by Helen Mitchell

page 245: courtesy Esther Woollaston, photography by Helen Mitchell

Index